BREAD MACHINE COOKBOOK FOR BEGINNERS

Unlock a Variety of Tasty Homemade Breads with 150 Simple and Stress-Free Recipes

BARBARA J. GILLIAM

Table of Contents

Introduction

A bread machine is a type of electronic counter-appliance used primarily for baking and making bread. While certain elements of bread makers may vary, most of them have common features.

For example, bread makers need between three and four hours to produce an ordinary white loaf, and they need up to four hours for a full meal loaf.
Moreover, you load the ingredients into the bread maker (either pre-mixed or by manually weighing the components), and the machine does the kneading and baking verification for you.

It is not, however, a quick procedure and requires at least three hours for each loaf. Due to the shape of the baking dish, loaves made at home seem more square-shaped than those purchased in stores, although they weigh around 800 grams on average, similar to the majority of loaves purchased in stores.

The majority of bread makers have a delayed timer that lets you fill it to the brim with all the ingredients and set it to bake for up to 13 hours.

This is especially advantageous if you want the bread maker to arrive overnight (electricity may occasionally be less expensive depending on the contract and supplier) and have a freshly baked loaf waiting for you when you wake up.

You may also utilise the breadmaker's kneading feature to generate pasta dough, roll dough, and pastry dough.

Bread makers vary greatly, some have more complicated cycles than others. Some bread machines are more expensive, but they are more useful kitchen appliances because of their cycles for cakes, loaves, preserves, desserts, sweet dough, and gluten-free baking.

A bread maker may do all of the steps in the process, including mixing, kneading, and baking. Proceed with only the ingredients placed in the machine's pan. In two or three hours, you'll be eating freshly cooked bread. However, this countertop device might potentially produce much more than simply bread loaves, such as doughnuts, hot dog buns, pizza crusts, and cinnamon rolls. It's simple to put a warm bread loaf or other delicacies on the table because many of the recipes only call for a few staple ingredients.

Chapter 1:

Introduction to Bread Machines

What is a Bread Machine?

After sliced bread, the freshly made bread is the greatest part!
The only issue is that it requires work and time.

The introduction of automated bread-making machines has started to impact the lives of many people who have never made bread and never will. Millions of people now convert their kitchens into bakeries and enjoy their own freshly made bread every day for a fraction of the price they would spend at a supermarket. What is the main advantage of bread-making appliances?

In what way and to what extent do they function?
You understand that making bread by hand is not a simple task. A lot of whisking, mixing, and kneading are needed. It may be rather painless to stir and knead bread dough that has been smoothed down with lots of butter and eggs. However, the

laborious labour involved might cause stiff dough. A bread processor will help in this situation.

A well-made bread processor will handle all the grubby physical labour and free you up to focus on your professional duties. Best of all, all you need to operate a bread machine as you choose is the ability to push a few buttons.

It's a good idea to become familiar with the features and capabilities of a bread machine before purchasing. Find out about the price range for these devices; depending on the type and features you choose, they can cost anywhere from less than $70 to more than $180.

There's a crust setting choice that lets you get mild, moderate, or darker dough on your bread loaf; some feature timings and latency controls, while others don't. The type of bread you want to make in your machine must also be known to you. Make sure the bread machine you choose has a loop for creating wheat bread if you're a huge fan of doing so. A separate loop for making cakes and jams is available on several bread machines. Make sure the bread maker you choose has all the features you need and enough cycles to meet your baking demands before making the purchase.

If you are unable to remove it when the baking process is over, it is a good idea to check for a cool-down cycle.

While many other machines provide a warm cycle to prevent sogginess, others have a tendency to dry up the bread.

A bread maker with several compartments could be a good idea, but it might also mean more effort and potential technical problems.

Bread makers that make loaf, square, round, and modern rectangles in a range of sizes and forms are available for purchase. How easy it is to remove the bread from a bread machine for cleaning is something else to consider. Checking for crumbs to accumulate is an excellent workout that keeps your bread machine safe. It's not always necessary to do so. After each use, I would advise against allowing the crumbs to accumulate.

The size is an important factor to take into account when purchasing any gadget for your kitchen. You should get a bread maker that fits your demands rather than one that occupies all of your additional kitchen space. Make sure to review all of the features to make sure they meet your requirements. Certain models on the market do not include instructions on how to use your bread machine, so be sure yours does. You have the choice to select the more costly or less expensive model but keep in mind that you get what you pay for.

The invention of the bread machine

Bread machines have introduced a new way of making bread, since busy chefs at home may have a nutritious and fresh addendum to home-made or conventional (non-home-made food). Bread making was a lucrative ability in ancient times because the method was labour-intensive, and it took several hours to make. A substantial number of employees were often working in early bakeries.

In the 1800s the first bread-processing machine was invented by Joseph Lee. His advent was a device capable of crumbling day-old bread for use in other treaties. Old bread had been dumped out leading up to his layout. Lee produced the first electric bread machine, using the money he earned from his first invention. The machine was able to blend and knead the dough, which enabled bakers to concentrate on the bread being formed and baked.

As well as accelerating the cycle of bread baking, Lee developed a more healthful approach to producing bread. Bakeries started buying the electric device to produce enough pieces of bread. Most bakeries used a bread maker during the 1950s. Unfortunately, it was not until 1986 that at-home chefs had access to the conventional machine.

The first bread machine capable of producing a single loaf was created by the Japanese manufacturing company Matsushita Electric, which is now known as Panasonic. After that machine gained popularity, other manufacturers started to build identical models. Every bread machine in use today has components from Joseph Lee's original design. Modern breadmaker manufacturers have figured out how to replicate the process employed by Lee's machine. The bread machine picks over and completes the preparation by creating the ideal loaf of bread when a busy cook loads the proper components into it. Most of the time, the chef has to put the liquid components into the unit first, and then the dry items. To guarantee that the liquid activates the quick yeast, the materials in the machine must be added in the correct order. Therefore, until the dough-making process starts, the water and the yeast must remain intact.

A bread machine's bread takes many hours to complete. Chefs will observe that the machine uses its paddle to move the materials to generate dough. Bread makers often maintain the ideal temperature, which promotes the best possible growth. The machine will begin baking the dough once it has been given the proper amount of time to rise.

Modern bread machines create loaves that feel conventional, unlike the strange shapes that older machines make. Using a bread maker might require chefs to adhere to a machine-designed recipe because it yields a smaller loaf than a traditional bread recipe.
Additionally, prepared bread mixes that come in the proper serving amounts are sold at supermarkets. All the chef had to do was stir in some water.

When making bread at home—from scratch or with a bread machine—cooks need to keep in mind that it won't survive as long as bread from the store since it won't include preservatives. In 1996, several families bought the machine, and ten years later, the majority of those claiming to possess bread makers had doubled. Manufacturers have quadrupled the machine's value by adding the ability to make baked goods, bread rolls, and pizza dough.

Customers who use the device regularly discover that a bread maker can prepare nearly any dough composition, which can then be cooked in a regular oven. Many recipe books with instructions for using bread makers have been released. A dedicated cook can now provide their family with a handmade supper that includes freshly baked bread thanks to the bread machine, which has become a modern household staple.

How does it work?

Numerous other features are included in certain bread makers, such as an embedded memory that allows them to continue operating after a brief power interruption (sometimes known as a "blackout") for a few minutes. A staggered launch is possible with many bread makers since you may add the ingredients right before bed and wake up in the morning to a freshly baked loaf. (It's important to note, too, that if you happen to leave a loaf in a hot machine after it's finished, the crust will continue to cook and become substantially tougher; this may or may not be to your liking.)

What's inside it?

- The folding lid has an incorporated baking tin cover.
- The steam exhaust vent is located in the centre of the folding, sliding lid.
- Steam may escape from the baking tin by passing through the lid and into the exhaust switch.
- Air can rise into the dough thanks to the air vent.
- lead for the power source.
- The centre of the tin has a hole where the electric axle that rotates the kneading paddle is securely hooked.

- During the process, the bread maker can safely come into touch with the oven thanks to the outer plastic cover that protects it.
- Simple touch panel control panel with LCD display for easy cleaning.
- the curving slot at the bottom where the lid locks in.
- One loaf can be baked in tandem with the detachable baking tin.
- The removable kneading snorkel is positioned across the centre of the tin and clicks on an axle within a watertight seal.
- To guarantee that heat is maintained, a tongue around the lid's edge at the lower portion of the machine puts further focus on the groove (9).

How to use it?

Bread-maker programming is a simple operation:
- Select a type of bread: pizza, whole wheat, multigrain, basic, or French.
- Select the bake option (dough, sandwich, bake rapid, and bake).
- The series of mixing, kneading, rising, and baking varies for each.
- For example, when the machine is in the dough mode, it stops before the dough is cooked. At this point, you lift the top, take

out the dough, and use it for pizza, croissants, or anything else you like. (The bread maker can assist you in cooking the dough; you will need to bake the ones in the oven.)

- Choose between the big, medium, or comparatively little loaf sizes.
- Decide on your preferred crust type.
- Select the TIMER button. The monitor shows how long it usually takes for the loaf to cook through.
- To begin the countdown to a tasty loaf, select the Start button!
- Once the loaf is baked, gently remove the cover (it should take anywhere from two to six hours, but generally about three to four), remove the hot tin from the oven, tilt the loaf, and allow it to cool. It just takes around 30 seconds to clean by simply rinsing away the paddle and the appropriately non-stick pan.

1.3 Types of Bread Machines/Makers

Most bread-making machinery might use some modification. This is because every alteration made to a bread machine has a specific purpose in mind. The bread machine models that are most popular worldwide are listed below.

Vertical

Since this is how the bread box was created, many bread machines make loaves that are arranged vertically. There is only one kneading paddle included with this kind of bread maker.

Horizontal

Several bread-making appliances have two kneading paddles within the pot. These bread makers, which resemble store-bought bread, bake bread horizontally.

Small

If your kitchen is small or you don't eat a lot of bread, a small bread maker is ideal. These little kitchen assistants only make enough bread for a couple or a person and don't take up much space in the kitchen.

Large

Large families may find that bread disappears quickly from the bread machine—especially when there are many guests at the table! Large bread machines may produce three pounds of bread. A large household may be sustained on loaves of bread.

Gluten-free bread machine

There are settings on a gluten-free bread maker specifically designed for this kind of diet. The complicated requirements of gluten-free components are addressed by the proper baking temperatures, time settings, and conditions that come with this breadmaker.

Using a bread machine instead of purchasing from bakeries is a more affordable and healthful choice for many individuals following a gluten-free diet. Additionally, they discover that producing their own gluten-free bread is far less expensive than buying commercially produced versions, which are sometimes offered at inflated costs due to their superior health.

Manufacturing companies

Let's examine the companies that produce bread makers. Even though there are hundreds of bread machine manufacturers in the globe, we'll concentrate on the most reputable and well-known ones.

Panasonic

You've probably heard of Panasonic before; it's a well-known brand that powers a number of gadgets.

Matsushita Electric Industrial Co., Ltd. was another name for Panasonic Corporation in the past. The company manufactures international Japanese electronics. The numerous amazing features that Panasonic bread machines offer allow them to maintain their position at the top of the market. Five bread machine models are available from Panasonic, one of which has a completely automated yeast dispensing mechanism.

Zojirushi

The Zojirushi Company is a Japanese corporation that makes different home appliances. One of the product categories of Zojirushi-bread makers.

This manufacturer's bread machines are known for their exceptional quality.

The company manufactures processors in two sizes which reflect the preferences of the customers. The 2-lb. Standard baking works best with the 2-pound bread machines. The 1-lb. The bread processor is a great option for someone who doesn't eat much bread.

West Bend

West Bend, Wisconsin Corporation was the name given to the West Bend Company from 1911 and 2001. The West Bend Company manufactured aluminium appliances and kitchenware.

It is also well-known for manufacturing outboard boat motors and other stroke cycle engines. With its wonderful experience behind it, West Bend Corporation is able to provide its customers high-end products. Known as West Bend Housewares, the West Bend Division of Simple Kitchen Appliance is well-known.

Breadman

The brand is an American one for kitchen appliances. The capacity to produce expertly prepared home-style bread is provided by Breadman bread makers. Outstanding quality and reliable customer service are hallmarks of the brand.

Breville

Australian company Breville was established in Melbourne in 1932 and produces tiny household appliances. In both New Zealand and the USA, the company has demonstrated that it uses premium materials in the production of its products.

Benefits of Bread Machines

Using a bread maker may seem like a silly idea to some, but for others, it's impossible to imagine living without freshly baked bread. Now let's get real: there are several advantages to having a bread machine.

- The freshly baked, homemade bread is the first thing you can taste.
- The ability to set a timer to bake at a certain level is another feature found on many bread makers. This feature comes in if you want to have freshly made bread for breakfast in the morning.
- Everything you consume can be fixed. Those who want to limit their intake of certain foods or those with allergies will find that preparing bread at home allows them to control exactly what ingredients go into their loaf.
- That is feasible. There is a misconception among many individuals that bread making at home is untidy and difficult. It could also be simple to bake bread in a bread maker. The bread machine does all of the mixing, rising, and baking for you—you only need to select the choice! It's also the least messy method!
- Long-term savings from this will be enormous. Perhaps you are incorrect in thinking that purchasing bread from a supermarket is less expensive. So, if you have

certain dietary requirements, baking bread at home will ultimately save you money.

- Several forms of bread, including Rye, whole wheat, gluten-free, and several more, may be produced using bread machines. Other delicious dishes that may be created include jam, pizza dough, pasta dough, and more.
- Both superior quality and good taste. It needs to be stated. Nothing beats the fresh bread's firmness and flavour. Being the bread maker, you can be certain that you utilise only the highest-quality, freshly-picked ingredients. Home-baked bread unquestionably surpasses store-bought food in terms of flavour and consistency.

The tasks performed by bread producers go beyond simply making different kinds of bread. We wish to explore some new uses for a bread maker down below. A bread machine is a really powerful culinary tool, according to industry expert Joy Crump. Foode is a farm-to-table café located in Fredericksburg, Va, where Mr. Crump serves as head chef. He was talking about how to make your breadmaker multitask.

Create the best tomato sauce in a bread machine

According to Mr. Crump, a bread machine is just as good as a crockpot. But in his opinion, the restlessness feature tends to make the bread maker perfect for using sauce.

Baking a Casserole

Instead of using a gas oven, a bread machine may be used to make any kind of casserole.

One may create their veggies or butter of fruit

According to Mr. Crump, the most effective way to bake apple butter is using a bread maker.

He said that the fruit develops sugars because of the slow heating within the bread machine.

Machines for bread can make cakes

The bread makers are the best ones for baking cakes, just like perfect bread loaves.

Types of Bread and Manufacturing

As the saying goes, "bread is the staff of life." Low-carb diets may attempt to eliminate it, but for the majority of us, it nonetheless exists.Although bread has been a staple of the human diet since the Neolithic era, some 10,000 years ago, it is true that it is heavy in carbohydrates. It tastes well and is reasonably priced, not to mention filling. For a very long time, a vast number of individuals have loved various types of bread. The basic technique used to bake bread hasn't changed over generations. The principal components are flour, salt, yeast, and water. There exist several types of bread, with numerous varieties unique to a particular area and culture. There have been 3 basic forms of bread in the globe: those that develop maximal and hence have to be baked in pans, bread with a moderate volume, such as rye & French bread, and others that hardly grow and are thus termed flatbreads.

Bread making involves a lot of steps. Some of the steps are not optional but some are. Bread production seems somewhat difficult, but it won't be as challenging anymore once you know why you'd want to take the various steps and have the resources to take the measures.

2.1 Bread Types and Their Origins

English muffin

It is a small, round, flat, leavened yeast bread that is usually toasted and cut horizontally. When it comes to tea time snacks, they're not a bad option, but it depends on what you put on them. Butter may be substituted with unsaturated spread, which is better for the heart. Wilted spinach with poached eggs on top of a muffin may make a delicious and nutritious breakfast; but, eggs Benedict with bacon, poached eggs, and Hollandaise buttery sauce are best saved for special occasions.

Tortilla

This is not wheat flour or maize meal; rather, it is a type of thin, soft flatbread. These bread are used in numerous Mexican cuisines like enchiladas, tacos burritos as well as wraps. Fajitas may be a healthy alternative with a few simple adjustments, but deep-fried chimichangas and enchiladas with an abundance of cheese are not to be ignored. To make their own healthy alternative, one can lightly spray tortillas with oil and bake them in the oven until crisp. Tortilla chips are pieces of tortilla that are deep-fried, often with additional salt and other seasonings along with them.

Soda bread

Ireland's traditional bread is called soda bread, and its essential components are baking soda, flour, salt, and buttermilk. Instead of using yeast as a leavening ingredient, baking soda is used. This will add sodium to the bread, and like with salt, using too much might raise blood pressure, so test the recipe with caution and just use what you need. Because Irish flour was likewise too soft to generate yeast, traditional Irish chefs used baking soda or bread soda instead of yeast. Making this bread doesn't need waiting for it to rise, making it simple and quick to prepare.

Whole Pitta Food

In the Middle East, nearly all dishes are served with pita bread. It is widely available in white and wholemeal varieties, and it may be used for sandwiches or as a dip. If you can, go for whole-grain bread in its whole meal form as it is a vital component of a balanced diet. With some reduced-fat veggies or hummus, wholemeal pitta makes a delicious snack or light dinner.

Injera

It's a unique, slightly spongy flatbread that has been made with sourdough. Teff, a tiny round grain that grows in the Ethiopian highlands, is traditionally used to make injera. Large injera are traditionally used to serve Ethiopian food. To pick up the toppings of meat stews and veggies, use this slightly soured flatbread.

Paratha

Indian whole-wheat flour is used to make paratha, a layered flatbread. It is popular as well in diverse nations including Burma, Malaysia, and Singapore. Due to its common cooking or frying in oil, ghee, or butter, as well as the possibility of further layering of ghee or butter, parathas are often heavy in fat. Baking parathas in the oven or cooking them in a tiny quantity of oil might be healthier options. These can occasionally be filled with a variety of ingredients, including eggs, potatoes, veggies, onions, and even seasonings.

Arepa

Typically consumed in Colombia and Venezuela, it is a flat, spherical patty made of cornmeal. It may be baked, fried or even cooked over a charcoal grill. Stuffing options include gammon, black beans, chicken salad, rubbed cheese, avocado, Perico (Venezuelan scrambled eggs), or thinly sliced beef. To create arepas, you'll need precooked corn flour, water and a small bit of salt. Because it is composed of cornflour, it is gluten-free.

Focaccia

Italian focaccia is a flatbread cooked in the oven with strong (high-gluten) wheat, water, oil, salt, and yeast. It might serve as sandwich bread, a basis for pizza, or an appetiser for a variety of dishes. It is typically seasoned with extra salt or has a topping of numerous other salty stuff like olives, be cautious to test this bread way too much. Make careful to read the food labels on the pack if you purchase this at the supermarket because it may be quite greasy, making it more in calories than other breads. Alternatively, try baking your own bread and flavouring it with fresh rosemary or tomato slices instead of adding salty toppings.

Roti

Roti is an unleavened flatbread that is popular across the Caribbean and almost all of India. It is similar to chapatti. Whole Wheat flour and water are combined to produce them, and they're frequently topped with butter or ghee to improve the flavour and maybe increase in calories. If your goal is to produce a bucket of roti, then you should only spread butter on the third or fourth roti rather than each one.

Even with significantly less fat, you will still be able to taste the flavour. Tandoori roti might be considered a healthful option because it is prepared in a tandoori oven. Snacking on roti stuffed with spices is common in many parts of the West Indies.

Lavash

This is a thin flatbread, popular in Iran, Turkey, and the Caucasus region, made in the Armenian manner.

Flour, water, and salt are used in its preparation. Because it is usually baked on a tandoori burner, lavash has little fat. Sometimes roasted sesame seeds or poppy seeds are added before baking. When lavash is new, it gets mushy and then dries till it becomes crisp.

Grissini

Grissini, which are pencil-sized, crisp, dry breadsticks, are thought to have come from Italy. They are crispy all over and may be seasoned to go well with anything else you serve with a range of herbs, spices, and seeds. For bread and butter and garlic toast at the start of a dinner, a few grissini would be a better option.

2.2 **History of Bread**

These are two of the earliest plants known to exist, and it is thought that early humans, dating back to 5000 B.C., ate these grains. People began experimenting with cooking the mixture of grain and water on tiny stones that were then cooked in the fire when it was discovered that adding water to the grain managed to make it more appetising.

This is how porridge and flatbread were made. It was generally known that barley was grown alongside wheat by the ancient Egyptians. Archaeological excavations in these cities revealed that they adored flatbreads with nearly every meal. Raised or leavened bread most likely happened by accident when a mixture of water and wheat was kept in a very warm setting, allowing the naturally occurring yeast to produce a puff dough. It's also possible that some of the leftover dough was mixed into a new batch, which would have had the same results. The bread received a far higher rating when the dough was prepared in an oven rather than over an open flame.

The first furnaces were made of clay and used wood to ignite fires. When the wood pieces were completely burnt, the embers were snagged out of an aperture at the edge of the oven. The oven's

aperture was shut once the wheat dough was placed inside.
By the time the furnace cooled down, the bread was done.

The practice of stroking grain between two stones to create grinding processes dates back to the Roman era. A mechanical mechanism that rotates a stone over a stationary stone that was both lower and perpendicular to it progressively replaced the hand grinding procedure. Originally, slaves or animals were used to turn the wheel of stones. Afterwards, water or wind mills supplied the electricity.

Indeed, grinding took a long time, and for generations, leavened bread was only enjoyed by the wealthy. White bread has been an incredibly scarce item. A family's bread consumption may have indicated their social and economic standing. The whole-grain (dark) bread was consumed by the most impoverished members of society.

Interestingly, whole-grain bread is now preferred above white flour bread by nutritionists. Even during the Middle Ages, bread production remained a purely domestic activity. During that period, some people—especially those without access to ovens—started bringing their dough to neighbourhood little bakeries to have it shaped and cooked. Home baking significantly decreased as cities and villages sprung up throughout the countryside, and bakeries proliferated. Large brick ovens fueled by coal or wood were present in these neighbouring bakeries. The dough was transferred into and out of the ovens using a long-handled, wooden shovel called a "peel."

Although many independent and small bakeries still utilise peel ovens, many have already been updated to run on gas or oil.

Since most people don't include bread in their daily diets, it was thought to be fattening, even for a little while. Nonetheless, research has indicated that a significant portion of the calories that led to fat development came from coatings or toppings like butter. But bread is also a great source of low-fat foods and complex carbs. Customers' tastes for a variety of bread varieties have been influenced by their increased interest in bread. White bread slices are not as common as they once were. Nowadays, a wide variety of wheat and multigrain breads are available on store shelves.

2.3 Bread Manufacturing

Bread is manufactured from 3 fundamental materials i.e. water, bakers' yeast, and flour.
According to the sort of bread that will be made, the gathered grain is ground. Germ, endosperm, and bran are the three primary components of all grains. Rye bread and whole-wheat bread are made from the three components. White flour cannot be made without removing the bran and germ. When it comes to nutrition, minerals and vitamins can "enrich" white flour because they comprise the majority of the grain's components in the germ and bran. There are also certain white flours that are calcium and protein-enriched. Grain factories handle the grinding and supply the grain in large quantities to bakers.

Up until it is ready for sale, the bakers keep the grain in stock bags. To create the dough, flour, water, and yeast are mixed in the baking factory. Fat, salt, sugar, raisins, honey, and nuts are among the additional components added by the factory.

The Manufacturing Process
1. Mixing & kneading the dough.
In an industrial blender, the refined flour is added. Water with temperature control In the blender, bread is pumped in. Known as "gluten," this

mixture provides the bread its elastic qualities. The yeast is already measured. Moreover, yeast is a tiny creature that usually consumes the sugars found in grains and produces carbon dioxide. The gas bubbles produced by the yeast development leaven the bread. Additional ingredients are added to the mixer based on the sort of bread that is intended to be made.

Up to 2,000 pounds (908 kg) of dough may be processed per minute using sophisticated mixers.
A closed container that turns at a speed of between 35 and 75 revolutions per minute is essentially what a blender is. The dough is kneaded to the appropriate consistency in a matter of seconds by electrical arms within the container.

The ability of the mixing workers to judge the dough's appearance and elasticity is crucial, even in this highly automated age of bread manufacture. Professional workers can judge the quality of the dough as it passes through the mixer based on the tone of the dough. It takes around twelve minutes to combine.

2. Fermentation

The fermentation of the dough is done using three methodologies. The high-speed machinery is engineered in some plants to modify the dough at very high speeds and with a massive force that compels the yeast cells to increase rapidly. The inclusion of added chemicals, like 1-cysteine and vitamin C, also can induce fermentation. Certain bread is naturally allowed to be fermented. The dough is put in wrapped metal bowls in this method and preserved in a temperature-controlled area till it rises.

3. Division & gas reproduction.

The dough is placed in a separator with rotating blades to cut it into predetermined portions when it has finished fermenting. The dough pieces are then transferred to a moulding machine using a conveyor belt. The dough is formed into balls by the moulding machine, which then places them into a stacked conveyor belt that is enclosed in a heated, humid storage area known as a "prover." The dough gradually passes through the prover to "rest," and the gas reproduction will continue.

4. **To mould & bake**.

After the dough is removed from the prover, it is sent through another moulding machine to reshape it into a loaf and place it in pans.

The pans are moved to the next prover, which is also set to a very high temperature and humidity. Here, the dough regains the elasticity that it lost throughout the fermentation process and the resting time. The pans reach a tunnel-oven from the prover. When the loaf comes out of the oven, the temperature and speed must be carefully calibrated so that they are fully cooked and relatively cooled. Inside the tunnel, the loaves are hand poured from pans onto the shelves. About 30 minutes are needed for the baking and chilling process.

5. **Slicing & packaging**.

As the bread moves from the oven to the slicer, it continues to cool. The bread is broken into uniformly shaped pieces by the vertical, sharp blades there, which move quickly up and down. While each loaf is picked up and sent to the wrapping unit, metal sheets hold the pieces together. Every loaf is automatically covered with pre printed bags. Certain bakeries use wire twists to close the packets. The packets are heat-sealed by other plants.

Perfect for Breakfast

1. Breakfast Bread Whole Wheat
Preparation Time: 5 minutes
Cooking Time: 3 hours 45 minutes
Servings: 14
Ingredients:

- 3 cups white whole wheat flour
- ½ teaspoon salt
- 1 cup water
- ½ cup coconut oil, liquified
- 4 Tablespoon honey
- 2½ teaspoon active dry yeast

Directions:

1. Follow the manufacturer's recommendations for temperature and order when adding ingredients to the bread machine.
2. Put the bread machine's top back on, choose the basic bread, medium crust option, and hit the start button.
3. Take out and place the bread on a cooling rack as soon as the bread maker is done baking.

Nutrition:
Carbs: 11 g
Fat: 3 g
Protein: 1 g
Calories: 60

2. Breakfast Bread Cranberry Orange

Preparation Time: 5 minutes

Cooking Time: 3 hours 10 minutes

Servings: 14

Ingredients:

- 1 1/8 cup orange juice
- 2 Tablespoon vegetable oil
- 2 Tablespoon honey
- 3 cups bread flour
- 1 Tablespoon dry milk powder
- ½ teaspoon ground cinnamon
- ½ teaspoon ground allspice
- 1 teaspoon salt
- 1 (.25 ounce) package active dry yeast
- 1 Tablespoon grated orange zest
- 1 cup sweetened dried cranberries
- 1/3 cup chopped walnuts

Directions:

1. Follow the manufacturer's suggested temperature and order of addition for each ingredient when adding it to the bread machine.
2. Shut the lid, choose the low crust, basic bread option on your bread maker, and hit the start button.
3. Add the chopped walnuts and cranberries five to ten minutes before the last kneading cycle concludes.

4. Take out the bread and place it on a cooling rack when the bread maker has completed baking.

Nutrition:

Carbs: 29 g

Fat: 2 g

Protein: 9 g

Calories: 56

3. Fluffy Paleo Bread

Preparation Time: 10 minutes
Cooking Time: 40 minutes
Servings: 15
Ingredients:

- One ¼ cup almond flour
- Five eggs
- 1 tsp. lemon juice
- 1/3 cup avocado oil
- One dash black pepper
- ½ tsp. sea salt
- 3 to 4 tbsp. tapioca flour
- 1 to 2 tsp. Poppyseed
- ¼ cup ground flaxseed
- ½ tsp. baking soda
- Top with:
- Poppy seeds
- Pumpkin seeds

Directions:

1. Preheat the oven to 350 F.
2. Place parchment paper inside a baking pan and set it aside.
3. Combine eggs, lemon juice, and avocado oil in a bowl and whisk to mix.

4. Combine the almond flour, baking soda, flaxseed, poppy seeds, black pepper, and tapioca flour in another bowl. Blend.
5. Mix well after adding the lemon juice mixture to the flour mixture.
6. Pour the batter into the loaf pan that has been prepared, then sprinkle more poppy and pumpkin seeds on top.
7. Place the loaf pan in the preheated oven, cover it, and bake for 20 minutes. After 15 to 20 minutes, remove the lid and bake until a knife inserted into the centre comes out clean.
8. Take it out of the oven and let it cool. Cut into pieces and serve.

Nutrition:

Calories: 149 Cal

Fat: 12.9 g

Carbohydrates: 4.4 g

4. Healthy Low Carb Bread

Preparation Time: 15 minutes
Cooking Time: 35 minutes
Servings: 8
Ingredients:

- 2/3 cup coconut flour
- 2/3 cup coconut oil (softened not melted)
- Nine eggs
- 2 tsp. Cream of tartar
- ¾ tsp. xanthan gum
- 1 tsp. Baking soda
- ¼ tsp. salt

Directions:

1. Preheat the oven to 350 F.
2. 2. Apply 1 to 2 tsp of grease to a loaf pan. Melted coconut oil and set it in the freezer to solidify.
3. Pour the eggs into a bowl and beat with a hand mixer for two minutes.
4. Stir the coconut oil into the eggs.
5. Transfer the dry ingredients into a second basin and stir to combine.
6. Add the dry ingredients to the egg mixture and use a hand mixer on low speed to mix until the mixture is mixed and dough is formed.

7. Fill the prepared loaf pan with the dough, place it in the oven, warm it to 350 degrees, and bake for 35 minutes.
8. Remove the bread pan from the heating element.
9. Cool, slice, and serve.

Nutrition:

Calories: 229

Fat: 25.5g Carb: 6.5g

Protein: 8.5g

5. Butter Bread Rolls

Preparation Time: 50 minutes
Cooking Time: 45 minutes
Servings: 24 rolls
Ingredients:

- 1 cup warm milk
- 1/2 cup butter or 1/2 cup margarine, softened
- 1/4 cup sugar
- 2 eggs
- 1 1/2 teaspoons salt
- 4 cups bread flour
- 2 1/4 teaspoons active dry yeast

Directions:

1. All ingredients should be added to a bread machine pan in the manufacturer's recommended sequence.
2. Choose the dough setting.
3. Turn the dough onto a surface that has been lightly floured when the cycle is finished.
4. Cut dough into twenty-four equal pieces.
5. Form dough into spheres.
6. Line a 13-by-9-inch baking sheet with cooking spray.
7. In a warm location, cover and allow to rise for 30 to 45 minutes.
8. Bake for 13 to 16 minutes at 350 degrees, or until golden brown.

Nutrition:
Carbs: 38 g
Fat: 2 g
Protein: 4 g
Calories: 18

6. Low-Carb Bagel

Preparation Time: 15 minutes
Cooking Time: 25 minutes
Servings: 12
Ingredients:

- 1 cup protein powder, unflavored
- 1/3 cup coconut flour
- 1 tsp. baking powder
- ½ tsp. sea salt
- ¼ cup ground flaxseed
- 1/3 cup sour cream
- 12 eggs
- Seasoning topping:
- 1 tsp. dried parsley
- 1 tsp. dried oregano
- 1 tsp. Dried minced onion
- ½ tsp. Garlic powder
- ½ tsp. Dried basil
- ½ tsp. sea salt

Directions:

1. Preheat the oven to 350 F.
2. Thoroughly mix the eggs and sour cream in a mixer.
3. In a bowl, combine the coconut flour, protein powder, baking powder, flaxseed, and salt.
4. Create a wet mixture by mixing the dry ingredients. Ascertain that it is thoroughly mixed.

5. In a separate dish, whisk together the spices for topping. Remove from the way.
6. Coat two doughnut pans, each holding six doughnuts.
7. After equally spooning batter into each, sprinkle the skillet with roughly 1 tsp of topping seasoning.
8. Using the remaining spice mixture, generously sprinkle each bagel on top.
9. Bake until golden brown, about 25 minutes.

Nutrition:

Calories: 134

Fat: 6.8g

Carb: 4.2g

Protein: 12.1g

7. Peanut Butter and Jelly Bread
Preparation Time: 2 hours
Cooking Time: 1 hour and 10 minutes
Servings: 1 loaf
Ingredients:

- 1 1/2 tablespoons vegetable oil
- 1 cup of water
- ½ cup blackberry jelly
- ½ cup peanut butter
- One teaspoon salt
- One tablespoon white sugar
- 2 cups of bread flour
- 1 cup whole-wheat flour
- 1 1/2 teaspoons active dry yeast

Directions:

1. Place the ingredients into the pan of your bread maker.
2. Go with the default configuration.
3. Press the Start button.
4. Once completed, remove the pan and leave it for ten minutes.

Nutrition:
Calories: 153 Cal
Carbohydrates: 20 g
Fat: 9g,
Cholesterol: 0mg
Protein: 4g
Fibre: 2g

Sugar: 11g
Sodium: 244 mg
Potassium: 120mg

8. Hot Dog Buns
Preparation Time: 10 minutes
Cooking Time: 50 minutes
Servings: 10
Ingredients:

- One ¼ cups almond flour
- 5 tbsp. psyllium husk powder
- 1 tsp. sea salt
- 2 tsp. baking powder
- One ¼ cups boiling water
- 2 tsp. lemon juice
- Three egg whites

Dircctions:

1. Preheat the oven to 350 F
2. Place all of the dry ingredients in a bowl and stir well.
3. Whisk together the dry ingredients with the boiling water, lemon juice, and egg whites.
4. Roll the ten sections of dough into buns using a mould.
5. Use the lowest oven rack to cook for 40 to 50 minutes after transferring to the preheated oven.
6. Remove it after making sure it's done.
7. Add the hot dogs and preferred toppings.
8. Serve.

Nutrition:
Calories: 104 |Fat: 8g |Carb: 1g |Protein: 4g

9. Spicy Bread
Preparation Time: 10 minutes
Cooking Time: 40 minutes
Servings: 6
Ingredients:
- ½ cup coconut flour
- Six eggs
- Three large jalapenos, sliced
- 4 ounces' turkey bacon, sliced
- ½ cup ghee
- ¼ tsp. baking soda
- ¼ tsp. salt
- ¼ cup of water

Directions:
1. Preheat the oven to 400F.
2. Place chopped bacon and jalapeños on a baking pan, then bake for 10 minutes.
3. After 5 more minutes of baking, flip.
4. Extract the jalapeño seeds.
5. In a food processor, combine the bacon pieces and jalapeños and pulse until smooth.
6. Combine eggs, ¼ cup water, and ghee in a bowl. Stir well.
7. After that, stir in some salt, baking soda, and coconut flour. Toss to combine.
8. Include the jalapeño mix and bacon.
9. Apply ghee to the loaf pan.
10. Transfer batter into a loaf pan.

11. Cook for 40 minutes. Appreciate.

Nutrition:

Calories: 240

Fat: 20g

10. Cranberry & Golden Raisin Bread

Preparation Time: 5 minutes

Cooking Time: 3 hours

Servings: 14

Ingredients:

- 1 1/3 cups water
- 4 Tablespoon sliced butter
- 3 cups flour
- 1 cup old-fashioned oatmeal
- 1/3 cup brown sugar
- 1 teaspoon salt
- 4 Tablespoon dried cranberries
- 4 Tablespoon golden raisins
- 2 teaspoon bread machine yeast

Directions:

1. 1. Following the directions provided by the manufacturer, add each ingredient—aside from cranberries and golden raisins—one at a time to the bread machine.
2. Close the cover, choose your bread machine's medium crust option (sweet or basic bread), and push the start button.
3. Five to ten minutes before the last kneading cycle concludes, add the golden raisins and cranberries.
4. Take the bread out of the bread maker and place it on a cooling rack when it has done baking.

Nutrition:
Carbs: 33 g
Fat: 3 g
Protein: 4 g
Calories: 175

11. Puri Bread

Preparation Time: 10 minutes

Cooking Time: 5 minutes

Servings: 6

Ingredients:

- 1 cup almond flour, sifted
- ½ cup of warm water
- 2 Tbsp. clarified butter
- 1 cup olive oil for frying
- Salt to taste

Directions:

1. Add the flour and salt to the water.
2. Pierce the dough in several places down the middle, then add melted clarified butter.
3. Knead the dough and cover and let it stand for 15 minutes.
4. Form into six balls.
5. Using a rolling pin, flatten the balls into six thin circles.
6. Heat up enough oil to thoroughly cover a circular skillet.
7. When it's hot, put a puri in it.
8. Fry each side for 20 seconds.
9. Lay out on a serviette.
10. Continue until all the puris are used, then serve.

Nutrition:

Calories: 106 |Fat: 3g |Carb: 6g |Protein: 3g

12. English muffin Bread

Preparation Time: 5 minutes

Cooking Time: 3 hours 40 minutes

Servings: 14

Ingredients:

- 1 teaspoon vinegar
- 1/4 to 1/3 cup water
- 1 cup lukewarm milk
- 2 Tablespoon butter or 2 Tablespoon vegetable oil
- 1½ teaspoon salt
- 1½ teaspoon sugar
- ½ teaspoon baking powder
- 3½ cups unbleached all-purpose flour
- 2 1/4 teaspoon instant yeast

Directions:

1. Follow the manufacturer's recommendations for temperature and order when adding ingredients to the bread machine.
2. Close the cover, turn on your bread machine to the basic bread, low crust option, and hit start.
3. Take out and place the bread on a cooling rack as soon as the bread maker is done baking.

Nutrition:

Carbs: 13 g |Fat: 1 g |Protein: 2 g |Calories: 62

Classic Bread

13. French Bread
Preparation Time: 2 Hours and 30 Minutes
Cooking Time: 30 Minutes
Servings: 14
Ingredients:
- 1 1/3 cups warm water
- 1 ½ tablespoon olive oil
- 1 ½ teaspoons salt
- Two tablespoons sugar
- 4 cups all-purpose flour; or bread flour
- Two teaspoons yeast

Directions:
1. Start your bread maker by adding warm water.
2. Add the sugar, salt, and olive oil in that order.
   Aim to adhere to that precise sequence. Stir in the flour after that.
   Cover the liquid ingredients completely.
3. Make a tiny indentation in the middle of the flour. Make sure the liquid is not touched by the indentation. In the indentation, place the yeast.
4. Press Start for the French Bread Cycle on the bread maker.

5. After kneading the dough for 5 minutes, assess it. Use ½ to 1 tablespoon of water to soften the dough if it's dry and stiff.
6. You can add 1 tablespoon of flour to the dough if it's too wet, until you get the desired consistency. Cut the bread after letting it cool for approximately 10 minutes.

Nutrition:

Calories: 121
Fibre: 1.1 g
Fat: 1.9 g
Carbs: 2.9g
Protein: 3.9 g.

14. White Bread

Preparation Time: 5 Minutes
Cooking Time: 3 Hours and 5 Minutes
Servings: 8
Ingredients:

- 1 cup of lukewarm water (110 degrees F/45 degrees C)
- Three tablespoons of white sugar
- 1 1/2 teaspoons of salt
- Three tablespoons of vegetable oil
- 3 cups of bread flour
- 2 1/4 teaspoons of active dry yeast

Directions:

1. 1. Fill the bread maker with yeast, water, sugar, salt, and oil.
2. 2. Bake on setting White Bread. Place it on wire racks to cool before slicing.

Nutrition:

Carbohydrates 3 g
Fats 5.6 g
Protein 9.6 g
Calories 319

15. Zojirushi Bread Machine Light Sourdough Bread

Preparation Time: 5 Minutes

Cooking Time: 25 Minutes

Servings: 8

Ingredients:

- Sourdough starter:
- 1 1/2 cups of water
- 2 cups (256 grams) of bread flour
- 2 tsp. of active dry yeast
- Bread Ingredients:
- 3 tbsp. of apple cider vinegar
- 2 tbsp. of lemon juice
- 3 cups of bread flour
- 1 tsp. of fine sea salt
- 2 tsp. of active dry yeast

Directions:

1. 1. Insert the bread pan into the Zojirushi Home Bakery Supreme bread maker along with the kneading blades.
2. Fill the bowl with bread flour and leaven.
3. Press Start after selecting a "sourdough starter" course. It should take about two hours to finish.
4. Everything is sparkling at the beginning.

For the bread.

5. When the sourdough starter beeps and terminates, press cancel to clear.

6. Add the ingredients listed, making sure to add the yeast on top of the flour.
7. Close the lid and programme a "basic" sequence.
8. After the bread bakes for just four hours, remove it and knock it out onto a cooling rack.
9. The bread can be frozen and sliced once it has cooled down for extended storage.

Nutrition:

Carbohydrates 3 g

Fats 5.6 g

Protein 9.6 g

Calories 319

16. Best-Ever Wheat Sandwich Bread

Preparation Time: 2 Hours

Cooking Time: 1 Hour

Servings: 6

Ingredients:

- 1-1/3 cups plus two tbsp. of light buttermilk
- Two tbsp. of dry milk
- Three tbsp. of local honey
- Two tbsp. of extra virgin olive oil
- 1-3/4 tbsp. of white whole wheat flour
- 2-1/4 cups of bread flour
- 2 tsp. of bread machine yeast

Directions:

1. Fill the bread maker with all of the ingredients in the specified order.
2. The yeast should be placed in a small well in the flour when using the delay timer so that it doesn't come into contact with any of the liquid below and you don't have to prepare the bread quickly.
3. The procedure should be carried out in compliance with the manufacturer's instructions.

Nutrition:

Carbohydrates 3 g

Fats 5.6 g

Protein 9.6 g

Calories 319

17. Homemade White Bread Less Dense

Preparation Time: 10 Minutes
Cooking Time: 3 Hours and 15 Minutes
Servings: 8
Ingredients:

- 1 cup and three tablespoons of water
- Two tablespoons of vegetable oil
- 1 1/2 teaspoons of salt
- Two teaspoons of sugar
- 3 cups of white bread flour
- Two teaspoons of active dry yeast

Directions:

1. Add oil and water to the bread pan. Add sugar and mix in the water.
   Pour flour into a pan.
2. Make sure that the ingredients do not come into touch with the flour by slightly indenting the surface of the flour. Apply the yeast to the indentation.
3. Avoid putting leaven in the water.
4. 4. Put the pan into the bread maker and press to seal it.
   Tighten the lid
5. Select the 1.5-pound loaf, medium crust, and basic bread settings (3 hours and 15 minutes).

6. Using oven mitts, take out the bread pan once it has baked.
   Shaking and turning the bread pan to allow the loaf to come out. Place the loaf on a wire rack and allow it to come to room temperature, for about 30 minutes.

Nutrition:

Carbohydrates 3 g

Fats 5.6 g

Protein 9.6 g

18. Softest Soft Bread with Air Pockets Using Bread Machine

Preparation Time: 15 Minutes
Cooking Time: 3 Hours and 20 Minutes
Servings: 8
Ingredients:

- 1 cup of lukewarm (105 to 115 degrees F/40 to 45 degrees C)
- Four teaspoons of honey
- Two teaspoons of active dry yeast
- 2 cups of all-purpose flour
- Four teaspoons of olive oil
- 1/2 teaspoon of salt

Directions:

1. Fill the pan of the bread maker with warm water, then sprinkle honey in the water until the honey dissolves. Before the yeast starts to bubble, add the yeast to the mixture and let it sit for about ten minutes. To the bread pan, add the flour, olive oil, and salt in the sequence recommended by the maker.
2. Choose a gentle setting if the machine offers that option; if not, use a regular setting and turn it on. Before cutting, allow the bread to cool.

Nutrition:
Carbohydrates 3 g
Fats 5.6 g

Protein 9.6 g
Calories 319

19. Hazelnut Honey Bread

Preparation Time: 3 Hours
Cooking Time: 30 Minutes
Servings: 10
Ingredients:

- ½ cup lukewarm milk
- Two teaspoons butter, melted and cooled
- Two teaspoons liquid honey
- 2/3 teaspoons salt
- 1/3 cup cooked wild rice, cooled
- 1/3 cup whole grain flour
- 2/3 teaspoons caraway seeds
- 1 cup almond flour, sifted
- One teaspoon active dry yeast
- 1/3 cup hazelnuts, chopped

Directions:

1. Get your measurement tools (a cup, a spoon, and kitchen scales) ready along with all the ingredients for your bread.
2. Add the ingredients, excluding the nuts and seeds, to the pan by carefully measuring them out.
3. Fill the bread bucket with all of the ingredients, making sure they are arranged correctly.
4. Next, proceed as directed by your bread machine's hand book.
5. Tighten the lid.

6. Toggle between the basic and medium crust colour settings on your bread maker.
7. Select "Start."
8. After the signal, incorporate the nuts and seeds into the dough.
9. Await the completion of the program.
10. When finished, remove the bucket and allow it to cool for a half hour to an hour.
11. Before letting it cool on a cooling rack for half an hour, give the loaf a shake in the pan.
12. Slicing, serving, and savouring the aroma of freshly baked bread.

Nutrition:

Carbohydrates 5 g

Fats 2.8 g

Protein 3.6 g

Calories 113

20. Cloud Savory Bread Loaf

Preparation Time: 10 Minutes
Cooking Time: 15 Minutes
Servings: 10
Ingredients:

- Six egg whites
- Six egg yolks
- 1/2 cup whey protein powder, unflavored
- 1/2 tsp. cream of tartar
- 6 oz. sour cream
- 1/2 tsp. baking powder
- 1/4 tsp. garlic powder
- 1/4 tsp. onion powder
- 1/4 tsp. salt

Directions:

1. Beat the egg whites until firm peaks form, adding the cream of tartar as needed. Put aside.
2. Transfer all remaining ingredients into a separate bowl and stir.
3. Gently fold the mixes in one half at a time.
4. Transfer mixture to pan in the bread maker.
5. Select "Quick Bread" on the bread maker.
6. Take the bread machine pan out of the bread machine after the bread is done.
7. Allow to cool a little bit before moving to a cooling bracket.

8. The bread can be stored on the counter for a maximum of three days.

Nutrition:

Calories: 90
Carbohydrates: 2g
Protein: 6g
Fat: 7g

21. Ciabatta Bread

Preparation Time: 15 Minutes

Cooking Time: 30 to 35 Minutes

Servings: 8

Ingredients:

- 1 1/2 cup water
- 1 1/2 teaspoon salt
- One teaspoon of white sugar
- One tablespoon of olive oil
- 3 1/4 cup bread flour
- 1 1/2 teaspoon bread machine yeast

Directions:

1. Using your stand mixer, combine all items except olive oil. Mix on low speed using a dough hook. Let it mix for ten minutes. If needed, scrape down the sides.
2. After adding the olive oil, mix for a further five minutes.
3. You want the dough to be quite sticky and wet, so resist the urge to add extra flour.
4. Place the dough on a lightly floured surface, cover it with a sizable bowl or greasy plastic wrap, and let it sit for fifteen minutes.
5. Use a light flour dusting or line baking sheets with parchment paper.

6. Divide the dough into two parts using a serrated knife and shape each piece into a 3×14-inch oval.
7. Transfer the loaves to the prepared sheets and sprinkle with flour.
8. Place a cover over the dough loaves and let them rise in a draft-free area for approximately 45 minutes.
9. Preheat the oven to 425 F.
10. Mist loaves with a little water.
11. Lay the loaves on the middle shelf of the oven.
12. Bake for about 25 to 35 minutes or until golden brown.
13. Serve.

Nutrition:
Carbohydrates 3 g
Fats 5.6 g
Protein 9.6 g
Calories 319

22. Almond Flour Bread

Preparation Time: 10 Minutes
Cooking Time: 10 Minutes
Servings: 10
Ingredients:

- Four egg whites
- Two egg yolks
- 2 cups almond flour
- 1/4 cup butter, melted
- 2 tbsp. psyllium husk powder
- 1 1/2 tbsp. baking powder
- 1/2 tsp. xanthan gum
- Salt
- 1/2 cup + 2 tbsp. warm water
- 2 1/4 tsp. yeast

Directions:

1. Combine all of the dry ingredients, excluding the yeast, in a small mixing bowl.
2. Place all of the wet ingredients in the pan of the bread machine.
3. Fill the bread machine pan with all of the dry ingredients that you removed from the lower mixing bowl. Add the yeast on top.
4. Select the basic bread option on the bread maker.
5. Take the bread machine pan out of the bread machine after the bread is finished.

6. Allow to slightly cool before transferring to a cooling rack.
7. You may keep the bread in the freezer for three months or for up to four days on the counter.

Nutrition:
Calories: 110
Carbohydrates: 2.4g
Protein: 4g
Fat: 10g

23. Bread Machine Olive Oil Bread
Preparation Time: 15 Minutes
Cooking Time: 3 Hours
Servings: 8
Ingredients:
- 1 cup of hot water
- 2 cups of white sugar
- 1.25 ounce of bread machine yeast
- 1/4 cup of olive oil
- 2 1/2 cups of bread flour
- 1/2 cup of whole wheat flour
- 1/2 tbsp. of salt

Directions:
1. Fill the bread machine basin with the water, sugar, and leaven. After 10 minutes of sitting, the yeast will melt and foam.
2. Fill the pot with oil, flour, and salt. Don't blend.
3. Select the White Bread setting on the bread maker and turn it on. (Baking takes roughly three hours.)
4. Savour it!

Nutrition:
Carbohydrates 3 g
Fats 5.6 g
Protein 9.6 g
Calories 319

24. Coconut Flour Bread
Preparation Time: 10 Minutes
Cooking Time: 15 Minutes
Servings: 12
Ingredients:

- Six eggs
- 1/2 cup coconut flour
- 2 tbsp. psyllium husk
- 1/4 cup olive oil
- 1 1/2 tsp. salt
- 1 tbsp. xanthan gum
- 1 tbsp. baking powder
- 2 1/4 tsp. yeast

Directions:

1. Combine the dry ingredients (except from the yeast) in a small mixing dish.
2. Pour all of the liquid ingredients into the pan of the bread maker.
3. Fill the bread machine pan with all of the dry ingredients from the small mixing bowl. Sprinkle the yeast over top.
4. Set the bread machine to the"Basic Bread" setting on the bread machine.
5. Take out the bread machine pan from the bread machine after the bread is done.
6. Before transferring to a cooling rack, let cool somewhat.

7. You can store bread in the freezer for three months or for up to four days when it is stacked on the counter.

Nutrition:

Calories: 174

Carbohydrates: 4g

Protein: 7g

Fat: 15g

25. Sandwich Buns

Preparation Time: 10 Minutes
Cooking Time: 25 Minutes
Servings: 8
Ingredients:

- Four eggs
- 2 ½ oz. almond flour
- 1 Tbsp. coconut flour
- 1 oz. psyllium
- 1 ½ cups eggplant, finely grated, juices drained
- 3 Tbsp. sesame seeds
- 1 ½ tsp. baking powder
- Salt to taste

Directions:

1. Mix grated eggplant with egg froth. Mix till frothy.
2. In another bowl, combine all of the dry ingredients.
3. In the third step, add them to the egg mixture. Blend well.
4. After lining a baking sheet with baking parchment, gently press the doughnuts into the shape with your hands.
5. Bake in the oven at 374°F for 20–25 minutes.

Nutrition:
Calories: 99 |Fat: 6g |Carb: 10g |Protein: 5.3g

26. Bread Machine Basic Bread - Easy as Can Be

Preparation Time: 5 Minutes
Cooking Time: 2 Hours and 20 Minutes
Servings: 1 Loaf
Ingredients:

- 1 cup (227 g) lukewarm water
- 1/3 cup (74 g) lukewarm milk
- Three tablespoons (43 g) butter
- 3 3/4 cups (447 g) Unbleached All-Purpose Flour
- Three tablespoons (35 g) of sugar
- 1 1/2 teaspoons salt
- 1 1/2 teaspoons of active dry yeast or instant yeast

Directions:

1. In the order recommended by the manufacturer, load all of the ingredients into your machine.
2. Press start after programming the basic white bread maker.
3. Remove the pan from the oven when a loaf is completed. After about five minutes, carefully shake the pan to loosen the loaf, and then slide it onto a cooling rack to finish cooling.
4. Store well-wrapped, four days on the shelf, or freeze for up to 3 months.

Nutrition:
Carbohydrates 3 g
Fats 5.6 g
Protein 9.6 g
Calories 319

27. Bread Machine Country White Bread

Preparation Time: 10 Minutes

Cooking Time: 2 Hours

Servings: 8 or 1 Loaf

Ingredients:

- 1 1/2 cups of water, lukewarm
- 2 1/2 cups of all-purpose flour
- 1 cup of bread flour
- 1/4 teaspoon of baking soda
- 2 1/2 teaspoons of a bread machine or instant yeast
- One tablespoon plus one teaspoon of olive oil
- 1 1/2 teaspoon of sugar
- One teaspoon of salt

Directions:

1. Fill your bread machine pan with all of the ingredients, following the order your bread machine manufacturer suggests.
2. Select the rapid or moderate setting, medium crust, and hit start.
3. Transfer the loaf to a shelf to cool.
4. Slice and enjoy!

Nutrition:

Carbohydrates 3 g

Fats 5.6 g

Protein 9.6 g

Calories 319

28. Bread Machine Peasant Bread

Preparation Time: 20 - 25 Minutes
Cooking Time: 25 Minutes
Servings: 1 Loaf
Ingredients:

- Two tablespoons of yeast
- 2 cups of white bread flour
- 1 1/2 tablespoon of sugar
- One tablespoon of salt
- 7/8 cup of water
- Topping of olive oil poppy seeds, sesame seeds, or cornmeal

Directions:

1. Follow the manufacturer's recommended order for mixing yeast, flour, sugar, salt, and water in the bread maker.
2. Select a typical bread and light crust setting.
3. After the bread has done baking, take it out of the oven and allow it to cool for five minutes. Place the bread on a cooling rack and drizzle a little olive oil over the top.
4. Finally, top with cornmeal, sesame seeds, or poppy seeds.
   Allow it to cool completely before cutting or storing.
5. 5. Freeze or store at room temperature in a closed container.

Nutrition:
Carbohydrates 3 g
Fats 5.6 g
Protein 9.6 g
Calories 319

29. Bread Machine Sandwich Bread

Preparation Time: 5 Minutes
Cooking Time: 25 Minutes
Servings: 8
Ingredients:

- 1 cup of heated water (45 degrees C)
- Two tablespoons of white sugar
- 2 1/4 teaspoon yeast
- 1/4 cup of olive oil
- 3 cups of bread flour
- 1 1/2 teaspoon salt

Directions:

1. In the pan of the bread maker, combine the yeast, sugar, and water.
2. After the yeast has been dissolved, let it foam for ten minutes.
3. Combine the flour, sugar, and salt with the yeast.
4. Press the Start button after selecting Basic settings. After three hours, the cycle is over.

Nutrition:

Carbohydrates 3 g

Fats 5.6 g

Protein 9.6 g

Calories 319

Sweet Bread

30. Chocolate Ginger and Hazelnut Bread
Preparation Time: 2 hours 50 minutes
Cooking Time: 45 minutes
Servings: 2 loaves
Ingredients:
- 1/2 cup chopped hazelnuts
- teaspoon bread machine yeast
- 1/2 cups bread flour
- 1 teaspoon salt
- 1 1/2 tablespoon dry skim milk powder
- tablespoon light brown sugar
- tablespoon candied ginger, chopped
- 1/3 cup unsweetened coconut
- 1 1/2 tablespoon unsalted butter, cubed
- 1 cup, plus 2 tablespoon water, with a temperature of 80 to 90
- degrees F (26 to 32 degrees C)

Directions:
1. Add the water, butter, coconut, candied ginger, brown sugar, milk, salt, flour, and yeast to the pan. Leave out the hazelnuts.
2. Close the cover and firmly insert the pan into the machine. Toasted hazelnuts should be added to the fruit and nut station.

3. Turn on the machine. Choose your preferred crust colour and basic setting, then hit the start button.
4. The baked bread should be gently moved to a wire rack to cool after baking.

Nutrition:

Calories: 273 calories;

Total Carbohydrate: 43 g

Total Fat: 11 g

Protein: 7 g

31. Chocolate Chip Bread

Preparation Time: 10 minutes

Cooking Time: 2 hours 50 minutes

Servings: 1 loaf

Ingredients:

- 1/4 cup water
- 1 cup milk
- 1 egg
- cups bread flour
- tablespoons brown sugar
- tablespoons white sugar
- 1 teaspoon salt
- 1 teaspoon ground cinnamon
- 1 1/2 teaspoon active dry yeast
- tablespoons margarine, softened
- 3/4 cup semisweet chocolate chips

Directions:

1. Fill the pan with all the ingredients, excluding the chocolate chips.
2. Choose mixed bread.
3. Insert the chips when the machine beeps.

Nutrition:

Calories: 184 calories;

Total Carbohydrate: 30.6 g

Cholesterol: 14 mg

Total Fat: 5.2 g

Protein: 3.5 g

Sodium: 189 mg

32. Buttery Sweet Bread

Preparation Time: 10 minutes
Cooking Time: 3 hours 40 minutes
Servings: 1 loaf
Ingredients:

- 1-Pound Loaf
- 1/3 Cup Milk
- 1/4 Cup Water
- 1 Large Egg
- Tablespoons Butter Or Margarine, Cut Up
- 3/4 Teaspoon Salt
- 2 1/4 Cups Bread Flour
- Tablespoons Sugar
- 1-1/2 Teaspoons Fleischmann's Bread Machine Yeast
- 1-1/2-Pound Loaf
- 1/2 Cup Milk
- 1/3 Cup Water
- 1 Large Egg
- 1/4 Cup Butter Or Margarine, Cut Up
- 1 Teaspoon Salt
- 3-1/3 Cups Bread Flour
- 1/4 Cup Sugar
- Teaspoons Fleischmann's Bread

Directions:

1 Put ingredients into a bread machine pan.

Nutrition:
Calories: 130 calories;
Total Carbohydrate: 17 g
Total Fat: 5 g
Protein: 3 g

33. Peanut Butter Bread
Preparation Time: 10 minutes
Cooking Time: 3 hours
Servings: 1 loaf
Ingredients:
- 1 1/4 Cups water
- 1/2 cup Peanut butter - creamy or chunky
- 1 ½ cups whole wheat flour
- tablespoons Gluten flour
- 1 ½ cups bread flour
- 1/4 cup Brown sugar
- 1/2 teaspoon Salt -
- ¼ teaspoons Active dry yeast

Directions:
1. Fill the pan with all of the ingredients.
2. Select the large loaf whole wheat bread setting.

Nutrition:
Calories: 82 calories;
Total Carbohydrate: 13 g
Cholesterol: 13 mg
Total Fat: 2.2 g
Protein: 2.5 g
Sodium: 280 mg
Fibre: 1 g

34. Hot Buttered Rum Bread

Preparation Time: 10 minutes
Cooking Time: 3 hours 40 minutes
Servings: 1 loaf
Ingredients:

- 1 egg
- 1 tablespoon rum extract
- tablespoons butter, softened
- cups bread flour
- tablespoons packed brown sugar
- 1 ¼ teaspoon salt
- 1/2 teaspoon ground cinnamon
- 1/4 teaspoon ground nutmeg
- 1/4 teaspoon ground cardamom
- 1 teaspoon bread machine or quick active dry yeast

Topping:

- 1 egg yolk, beaten
- 1 ½ teaspoon finely chopped pecans
- 1 ½ teaspoon packed brown sugar

Directions:

1. Break the egg into a cup, then fill the measuring cup with water.
2. Fill a pan with the egg mixture and bread ingredients.
3. Select a basic bread setting and a medium- to light-coloured crust.

4. With 40 to 50 minutes left in the cooking process, mix the topping ingredients in a small bowl and brush the mixture over the baked bread.

Nutrition:
Calories: 170 calories;
Total Carbohydrate: 31 g
Cholesterol: 25 mg
Total Fat: 2.0 g
Protein: 4 g
Sodium: 270 mg
Fibre: 1 g

35. Sweet Lemon Bread

Preparation Time: 3 hours
Cooking Time: 40 minutes
Servings: 6
Ingredients:

- oz. lemon zest, minced
- oz. of warm water (110-120 °F)
- 25 oz. wheat flour
- teaspoon instant yeast
- tablespoon olive oil
- oz. sugar

Directions:

1. Mix the sugar and yeast in a bowl until a smooth consistency is achieved by melting them both in the warm water.
2. After 20 minutes, mix the sifted wheat flour, olive oil, and yeast mixture.
3. Using a food processor, spiral mixer, or dough mixer, combine the zest of the lemon with the dough.
4. Transfer the dough into the bread maker and use water or egg yolk to moisten the dough's surface.
5. At this point, shut the cover and select the basic/white bread setting for the bread maker.

6. When the bread is done, remove it from the oven and cover it with a towel for one hour before consuming it.

Nutrition:

Calories: 69 calories;

Total Carbohydrate: 6 g

Total Fat: 4 g

Protein: 3 g

36. **Brownie Bread**

Preparation Time: 1 hour 15 minutes
Cooking Time: 50 minutes
Servings: 1 loaf
Ingredients:

- 1 egg
- 1 egg yolk
- 1 teaspoon Salt
- 1/2 cup boiling water
- 1/2 cup cocoa powder, unsweetened
- 1/2 cup warm water
- 1/2 teaspoon Active dry yeast
- tablespoon Vegetable oil
- teaspoon White sugar
- 2/3 cup white sugar
- cups bread flour

Directions:

1. In a small bowl, place the cocoa powder. To dissolve the cocoa powder, add hot water.
2. Transfer the yeast, 2 tsp white sugar, and warm water to a separate basin. Let the sugar and yeast dissolve. After the mixture becomes creamy, let it stand for roughly ten minutes.
3. Put in the bread pan with the cocoa mix, yeast mix, flour, vegetable, egg, and 2/3 cup white sugar. Pick the fundamental bread cycle. Press the START button.

Nutrition:
Calories: 70 Cal
Fat : 3 g
Carbohydrates: 10 g
Protein: 1 g

37. White Chocolate Bread

Preparation Time: 3 hours
Cooking Time: 15 minutes
Servings: 12
Ingredients:

- 1/4 cup warm water
- 1 cup warm milk
- 1 egg
- 1/4 cup butter, softened
- cups bread flour
- tablespoons brown sugar
- tablespoons white sugar
- 1 teaspoon salt
- 1 teaspoon ground cinnamon
- 1 (.25 oz.) package active dry yeast
- 1 cup white chocolate chips

Directions:

1. Ingredients should be added to the bread machine pan in the manufacturer's recommended order, excluding the white chocolate chips. Press the Start button to start the machine after selecting a cycle. If you are using a machine with a Fruit setting, add the white chocolate chips at the signal or up to 5 minutes before the kneading cycle is finished.

Nutrition:

Calories: 277 calories;

Total Carbohydrate: 39 g
Cholesterol: 30 mg
Total Fat: 10.5 g
Protein: 6.6 g
Sodium: 253 mg

38. **Almond and Chocolate Chip Bread**
Preparation Time: 10 minutes
Cooking Time: 3 hours 40 minutes
Servings: 1 loaf
Ingredients:
- 1 cup plus 2 tablespoons water tablespoons butter or margarine, softened
- ½ teaspoon vanilla
- cups Gold Medal™ Better for Bread™ flour
- ¾ cup semisweet chocolate chips tablespoons sugar
- 1 tablespoon dry milk
- ¾ teaspoon salt
- 1 ½ teaspoons bread machine or quick active dry yeast
- 1/3 cup sliced almonds

Directions:
1. Measure and add to the bread machine pan with all ingredients except almonds. 5 to 10 minutes before the kneading cycle stops, or at the Nut indication, add the almonds.
2. 2 Select the White cycle. Apply a little shade of crust colour.
3. Remove from the pan the baked bread.

Nutrition:
Calories: 130 calories;
Total Carbohydrate: 18 g
Total Fat: 7 g

Protein: 1 g
Protein: 3 g

39. Chocolate Chip Peanut Butter Banana Bread

Preparation Time: 25 Minutes
Cooking Time: 10 Minutes
Servings: 12 to 16 slices
Ingredients:

- Two bananas, mashed
- Two eggs, at room temperature
- 1/2 cup melted butter, cooled
- Two tablespoons milk, at room temperature
- One teaspoon pure vanilla extract
- cups all-purpose flour
- 1/2 cup sugar
- 11/4 teaspoons baking powder
- 1/2 teaspoon baking soda
- 1/2 teaspoon salt
- 1/2 cup peanut butter chips
- 1/2 cup semisweet chocolate chips

Directions:

1. In the bucket used for the bread machine, combine the bananas, eggs, butter, milk, and vanilla, set aside.
2. Combine the flour, sugar, baking soda, baking powder, salt, and chocolate and peanut butter chips in a medium-sized bowl.
3. Fill the bucket with the dry ingredients.
4. Select Quick/Rapid bread from the machine's menu and hit Start.

5. 5 After the cake is baked, test it with a knife to see whether it comes out clean. whether it does, the loaf is done.
6. Check the control panel for a Bake Only button and increase the duration by 10 minutes if the loaf requires a few more minutes.
7. Take the bucket out of the machine after the bread is finished.
8. Give the bread five minutes to cool.
9. Remove the bread from the can by gently rocking it, then place it onto a cooling rack.

Nutrition:

Calories: 297

Total Fat: 14g

Saturated Fat: 7g

Carbohydrates: 40g

Fibre: 1g

Sodium: 255mg

Protein: 4g

40. Cinnamon Raisin Bread

Preparation Time: 5 minutes
Cooking Time: 3 hours
Servings: 1 loaf
Ingredients:

- 1 cup water
- tablespoons margarine
- cups flour
- tablespoons sugar
- 1 1/2 teaspoons salt
- 1 teaspoon cinnamon
- 1/2 teaspoons yeast
- 3/4 cup raisins

Directions:

1. Combine all ingredients (except raisins) in the pan.
2. Select the sweet bread setting.
3. Put the raisins in after the machine beeps.

Nutrition:

Calories: 141 calories;
Total Carbohydrate: 26 g
Cholesterol: 00 mg
Total Fat: 2 g
Protein: 3.5 g
Sodium: 329 mg
Fibre: 1 g

41. Chocolate Sour Cream Bread

Preparation Time: 25 Minutes
Cooking Time: 10 Minutes
Servings: 12 slices
Ingredients:

- 1 cup sour cream
- Two eggs, at room temperature
- 1 cup of sugar
- 1/2 cup (1 stick) butter, at room temperature
- 1/4 cup plain Greek yoghourt
- 13/4 cups all-purpose flour
- 1/2 cup unsweetened cocoa powder
- 1/2 teaspoon baking powder
- 1/2 teaspoon salt
- 1 cup milk chocolate chips

Directions:

1. Gently stir together the sour cream, eggs, sugar, butter, and yoghurt in a small bowl until well blended.
2. Pour the moist ingredients into the bread machine bucket and stir in the flour, baking powder, cocoa powder, chocolate chips, and salt.
3. Select Quick/Rapid bread from the machine's menu and hit Start.
4. Test the loaf with a knife inserted into the centre; if it comes out clean, the loaf is done.

5. Check the control panel for a 'Bake Only' button and increase the duration by 10 minutes if the loaf requires a few more minutes.
6. After the bread is finished, take the bucket out of the machine.
7. Allow the bread to cool for half an hour.
8. Remove the loaf from the container with gentle rocking motions, then transfer it to a cooling rack.

Nutrition:

Calories: 347
Total Fat: 16g
Saturated Fat: 9g
Carbohydrates: 48g
Fibre: 2g
Sodium: 249 mg
Protein: 6g

42. Black Forest Bread

Preparation Time: 2 hour 15 minutes
Cooking Time: 50 minutes
Servings: 1 loaf
Ingredients:

- 1 1/8 cups Warm water
- 1/3 cup Molasses
- 1 1/2 tablespoons Canola oil
- 1 1/2 cups Bread flour
- 1 cup Rye flour
- 1 cup Whole wheat flour
- 1 1/2 teaspoons Salt
- tablespoons Cocoa powder
- 1 1/2 tablespoons Caraway seeds
- teaspoons Active dry yeast

Directions:

1. Fill your bread maker with all of the ingredients as directed by the manufacturer.
2. Choose a light crust type.
3. Select the start button.
4. When you begin to knead, don't forget to check.
5. Add a tablespoon of warm water at a time to the mixture if it's too dry.
6. Add flour again, a little at a time, if the mixture is too wet.
7. The mixture should form a ball and feel slightly sticky to the touch when applied to

the fingers. This applies to kneading all varieties of bread.

Nutrition:

Calories: 240 Cal

Fat: 4 g

Carbohydrates: 29 g

Protein: 22 g

43. Sweet Pineapples Bread

Preparation Time: 2 hours
Cooking Time: 40 minutes
Servings: 5
Ingredients:

- oz. dried pineapples
- oz. raisins
- oz. wheat flour
- eggs
- teaspoon baking powder
- oz. brown sugar
- oz. sugar
- Vanilla

Directions:

1. Soak the raisins in the warm water for 20 minutes.
2. 2 Add the vanilla, brown sugar, baking powder, and sifted wheat flour to a bowl.
3. Include the pineapples and raisins and combine well.
4. Using a whisk, beat the eggs and sugar together until the mixture is smooth and creamy.
5. Mix the flour mixture and dry fruit combination with the egg mixture.
6. Transfer the dough into the bread maker, shut the cover, and select the basic/white bread setting.

7. Once the bread reaches a medium crust, remove it from the oven and cover it with a cloth for one hour. Only then may you slice it.

Nutrition:

Calories: 144 calories;

Total Carbohydrate: 18 g

Total Fat: 9 g

Protein: 6 g

44. Apple Butter Bread

Preparation Time: 5 Minutes
Cooking Time: 25 Minutes
Servings: 8 slices
Ingredients:

- 2/3 cup milk
- 1/3 cup apple butter, at room temperature
- Four teaspoons melted butter, cooled
- Two teaspoons honey
- 2/3 teaspoon salt
- 2/3 cup whole-wheat flour
- 11/2 cup white bread flour
- One teaspoon of instant yeast

Directions:

1. Fill your bread maker with the ingredients according to the manufacturer's instructions.
2. Select light or medium crust, programme the system to run on Basic, and press Start.
3. Take the bucket out of the machine after the bread is finished.
4. Give the bread five minutes to cool.
5. To remove the loaf and place it on a rack to cool, gently shake the bucket.
6. Ingredient tip: Making apple butter in a slow cooker only requires a small amount of effort and cleanup. You can be confident of the ingredients in this delicious spread if you make your own.

Nutrition:
Calories: 178
Total Fat: 3g
Saturated Fat: 2g
Carbohydrates: 34g
Fibre: 1g
Sodium: 220mg
Protein: 4g

45. Apple Cider Bread

Preparation Time: 5 Minutes
Cooking Time: 25 Minutes
Servings: 8 slices
Ingredients:

- 1/4 cup milk
- Two tablespoons apple cider, at room temperature
- Two tablespoons sugar
- Four teaspoons melted butter, cooled
- One tablespoon honey
- 1/4 teaspoon salt
- cups white bread flour
- 3/4 teaspoons bread machine or instant yeast
- 2/3 apple, peeled, cored, and finely diced

Directions:

1. As directed by the manufacturer, put the ingredients into your bread machine, except the apple.
2. Press Start, choose Light or Medium Crust, then programme the machine for Basic/White bread.
3. 3. Add the apple 5 minutes before the final kneading cycle ends, or when the machine signals.
4. Take out the bucket from the machine after the loaf is finished.

5. Allow five minutes for the bread to cool.
6. Spoon the bread out onto a cooling rack after giving the bucket a gentle shake.
7. To ensure a beautiful rise in your bread, look for apple cider that has been well-spiced and sweetened.

Nutrition:

Calories: 164
Total Fat: 3g
Saturated Fat: 1g
Carbohydrates: 31g

46. Sweet Coconut Bread

Preparation Time: 2 hours
Cooking Time: 40 minutes
Servings: 6
Ingredients:

- oz. shredded coconut
- oz. walnuts, ground
- oz. wheat flour
- oz. coconut butter
- eggs
- teaspoon baking powder
- oz. brown sugar
- Vanilla

Directions:

1. Beat the eggs until they are creamy and smooth.
2. Add the eggs and thoroughly mix the coconut butter, brown sugar, and vanilla.
3. Mix the eggs, baking powder, and sifted wheat flour thoroughly until a smooth consistency is achieved.
4. Add the walnuts and shredded coconut to the dough, and thoroughly combine.
5. Transfer the dough into the bread maker, shut the cover, and select the basic/white bread setting.
6. Once the bread reaches a medium crust, remove it from the oven and cover it with a

cloth for one hour. Only then may you slice it.

Nutrition:

Calories: 164 calories;

Total Carbohydrate: 12 g

Total Fat: 8 g

Protein: 7 g

47. **Sweet Almond Anise Bread**

Preparation Time: 2 hours 20 minutes
Cooking Time: 50 minutes
Servings: 1 loaf
Ingredients:

- ¾ cup water
- ¼ cup butter
- ¼ cup sugar
- ½ teaspoon salt
- cups bread flour
- 1 teaspoon anise seed
- teaspoons active dry yeast
- ½ cup almonds, chopped

Directions:

1. Carefully follow the manufacturer's directions and add all of the ingredients to your bread maker.
2. Select Basic/White Bread as the bread machine's programme, and Medium for the crust type.
3. Press the START button.
4. Hold off until the cycle is finished.
5. After the bread is done, remove the bucket and allow it to cool for 5 minutes.
6. Shake the bucket gently to extract the loaf.
7. Move to a cooling rack, cut, and proceed to serve.
8. Have fun!

Nutrition:
Calories: 87 Cal
Fat: 4 g
Carbohydrates: 7 g
Protein: 3 g
Fibre: 1 g

48. Sour Cream Maple Bread

Preparation Time: 5 Minutes
Cooking Time: 10 Minutes
Servings: 8 slices
Ingredients:

- Six tablespoons water, at 80°F to 90°F
- Six tablespoons sour cream, at room temperature
- 1 1/2 tablespoons butter, at room temperature
- ¾ tablespoon maple syrup
- ½ teaspoon salt
- 1 3/4 cups white bread flour
- 1 1/6 teaspoons bread machine yeast

Directions:

1. Fill your bread maker with the ingredients according to the manufacturer's instructions.
2. Set the machine to make white or basic bread.
3. Press Start after selecting either light or medium crust.
4. Take the bucket out of the machine once the bread is finished.
5. Give the bread 5 minutes to cool.
6. Shake the pan gently to remove the loaf, then slide it out onto a cooling rack.

Nutrition:
Calories: 149

Total Fat: 4g
Saturated Fat: 3g
Carbohydrates: 24g
Fibre: 1g
Sodium: 168 mg
Protein: 4g

49. Barmbrack Bread

Preparation Time: 10 Minutes
Cooking Time: 25 Minutes
Servings: 8 slices
Ingredients:

- 2/3 cup water
- One tablespoon melted butter cooled
- Two tablespoons sugar
- Two tablespoons skim milk powder
- One teaspoon salt
- One teaspoon dried lemon zest
- 1/4 teaspoon ground allspice
- 1/8 teaspoon ground nutmeg
- cups of white bread flour
- 1 1/2 teaspoons bread machine or active dry yeast
- 1/2 cup dried currants

Directions:

1. Follow the manufacturer's instructions and load the ingredients into your bread machine, excluding the currants.
2. Press Start after setting the system to Basic and choosing between light and medium crust.
3. When your machine indicates or the second kneading cycle begins, add the currants.
4. Take the bucket out of the machine after the bread is finished.

5. Give the bread five minutes to cool.
6. To remove the bread, carefully sway the bucket and place it on a cooling rack.

Nutrition:

Calories: 175
Total Fat: 2g
Saturated Fat: 1g
Carbohydrates: 35g
Fibre: 1g
Sodium: 313 mg
Protein: 5g

50. **Honey Granola Bread**

Preparation Time: 5 Minutes

Cooking Time: 25 Minutes

Servings: 8 slices

Ingredients:

- 3/4 cups milk
- Two tablespoons honey
- One tablespoon butter, melted and cooled
- 3/4 teaspoons salt
- 1/2 cup whole-wheat flour
- 1/2 cup prepared granola, crushed
- 11/4 cup white bread flour
- One teaspoon of instant yeast

Directions:

1. Fill your bread maker with the ingredients according to the manufacturer's instructions.
2. Choose light or medium crust, programme the device for Basic/White bread, and tap Start.
3. Take the bucket out of the machine after the bread is finished.
4. Give the bread 5 minutes to cool.
5. Carefully shake the bucket to extract the loaf, then transfer it to a cooling rack.
6. Tip for the ingredients: Since you'll be smashing the granola for this recipe, opt for one without dried fruit. Dried fruit would

make the dough lumpy and ruin the texture
of the final bread.

Nutrition:

Calories: 151
Total Fat: 5g
Saturated Fat: 2g
Carbohydrates: 33g
Fibre: 2g
Sodium: 218mg
Protein: 6g

Spice and Herb Bread

51. Garlic Bread

Preparation Time: 2 hours 30 minutes

Cooking Time: 40 minutes

Servings: 1 loaf

Ingredients:

- 1 3/8 cups water
- tablespoons olive oil
- 1 teaspoon minced garlic
- cups bread flour
- tablespoons white sugar
- teaspoons salt
- 1/4 cup grated Parmesan cheese
- 1 teaspoon dried basil
- 1 teaspoon garlic powder
- tablespoons chopped fresh chives
- 1 teaspoon coarsely ground black pepper
- 1/2 teaspoons bread machine yeast

Directions:

1. Place the ingredients in the bread machine pan according to the manufacturer's recommended order.
2. Select the machine's Basic or White Bread cycle and hit the Start button.

Nutrition:

Calories: 175 calories;

Total Carbohydrate: 29.7 g

Cholesterol: 1 mg
Total Fat: 3.7 g
Protein: 5.2 g
Sodium: 332 mg

52. Cardamon Bread

Preparation Time: 2 hours
Cooking Time: 15 minutes
Servings: 8
Ingredients:

- ½ cup milk, at 80°F to 90°F
- 1 egg, at room temperature
- 1 teaspoon melted butter, cooled
- teaspoons honey
- ⅔ Teaspoon salt
- ⅔ Teaspoon ground cardamom
- cups white bread flour
- ¾ teaspoon bread machine or instant yeast

Directions:

1. Fill your bread maker with the ingredients according to the manufacturer's instructions.
2. Choose light or medium crust, programme the machine for Basic/White bread, and tap Start.
3. Take the bucket out of the machine after the bread is finished.
4. Give the bread 5 minutes to cool.
5. To remove the loaf, gently shake the bucket and place it onto a cooling rack.

Nutrition:

Calories: 149 calories;
Total Carbohydrate: 29 g
Total Fat: 2g

Protein: 5 g
Sodium: 211 mg
Fibre: 1 g

53. Spicy Cajun Bread

Preparation Time: 2 hours

Cooking Time: 15 minutes

Servings: 8

Ingredients:

- ¾ cup water, at 80°F to 90°F
- 1 tablespoon melted butter, cooled
- teaspoons tomato paste
- 1 tablespoon sugar
- 1 teaspoon salt
- tablespoons skim milk powder
- ½ tablespoon Cajun seasoning
- ⅛ teaspoon onion powder
- cups white bread flour
- 1 teaspoon bread machine or instant yeast

Directions:

1. Fill your bread maker with the ingredients according to the manufacturer's instructions.
2. Choose light or medium crust, programme the machine for Basic/White bread, and tap Start.
3. Take the bucket out of the machine after the bread is finished.
4. Give the loaf 5 minutes to cool.
5. To remove the loaf, gently shake the bucket and place it onto a cooling rack.

Nutrition:

Calories: 141 calories;

Total Carbohydrate: 27 g
Total Fat: 2g
Protein: 4 g
Sodium: 215 mg
Fibre: 1 g

54. Cumin Bread

Preparation Time: 3 hours 30 minutes
Cooking Time: 15 minutes
Servings: 8
Ingredients:

- 1/3 cups bread machine flour, sifted
- 1½ teaspoon kosher salt
- 1½ Tablespoon sugar
- 1 Tablespoon bread machine yeast
- 1¾ cups lukewarm water
- Tablespoon black cumin
- Tablespoon sunflower oil

Directions:

1. Fill the pan with all the dry and liquid ingredients, then proceed with your bread machine's directions.
2. Choose MEDIUM for the crust type and BASIC for the baking programme.
3. Modify the recipe's flour and liquid measurements if the dough is excessively thick or moist.
4. After the programme is done, remove the pan from the bread maker and allow it to cool for five minutes.
5. Give the loaf a shake to remove it from the pan. Use a spatula if required.
6. After wrapping the bread in a kitchen towel, leave it alone for one hour.

If not, a wire rack will work to cool it.

Nutrition:

Calories: 368 calories;

Total Carbohydrate: 67.1 g

Cholesterol: 0 mg

Total Fat: 6.5 g

Protein: 9.5 g

Sodium: 444 mg

Sugar: 2.5 g

55. Oregano Mozza-Cheese Bread

Preparation Time: 2 hours 50 minutes
Cooking Time: 50 minutes
Servings: 2 loaves
Ingredients:

- 1 cup (milk + egg) mixture
- ½ cup mozzarella cheese
- 2¼ cups flour
- ¾ cup whole grain flour
- tablespoons sugar
- 1 teaspoon salt
- teaspoons oregano
- 1½ teaspoons dry yeast

Directions:

1. Place all the ingredients into your bread maker.
2. Select Basic/White Bread from the programme on your bread machine, and then select Dark Crust.
3. Press START.
4. Wait until the entire cycle is over.
5. Remove the bucket when the loaf is done and allow it to cool for five minutes.
6. Shake the bucket carefully to remove the bread.
7. Move to a cooling rack, cut, and proceed to serve.

Nutrition:
Calories: 209 Cal
Fat: 2.1 g
Carbohydrates: 40 g
Protein: 7.7 g
Fibre: 1 g

56. Rosemary Bread

Preparation Time: 2 hours 10 minutes
Cooking Time: 50 minutes
Servings: 1 loaf
Ingredients:

- ¾ cup + 1 tablespoon water at 80 degrees F
- 1 ⅔ tablespoons melted butter, cooled
- teaspoons sugar
- 1 teaspoon salt
- 1 tablespoon fresh rosemary, chopped
- cups white bread flour
- 1 ⅓ teaspoons instant yeast

Directions:

1. Carefully follow the manufacturer's directions and add all the ingredients to your bread maker.
2. Select the Basic/White Bread programme on your bread maker and the Medium crust type.
3. Press the START button.
4. Wait until the entire cycle is finished.
5. After the loaf is done, remove the bucket and allow the bread to cool for 5 minutes.
6. To take out the bread, gently shake the bucket.
7. After transferring to a cooling rack, cut into slices and serve.

Nutrition:
Calories: 142 Cal
Fat : 3 g
Carbohydrates: 25 g
Protein: 4 g
Fibre: 1 g

57. **Lovely Aromatic Lavender Bread**
Preparation Time: 2 hours 10 minutes
Cooking Time: 50 minutes
Servings: 1 loaf
Ingredients:

- ¾ cup milk at 80 degrees F
- 1 tablespoon melted butter, cooled
- 1 tablespoon sugar
- ¾ teaspoon salt
- 1 teaspoon fresh lavender flower, chopped
- ¼ teaspoon lemon zest
- ¼ teaspoon fresh thyme, chopped
- cups white bread flour
- ¾ teaspoon instant yeast

Directions:

1. Carefully follow the manufacturer's directions and add all the ingredients to your bread maker.
2. Select the Basic/White Bread programme on your bread maker and the Medium crust type.
3. Press the START button.
4. Wait until the entire cycle is finished.
5. After the loaf is done, remove the bucket and allow the bread to cool for 5 minutes.
6. To take out the bread, gently shake the bucket.

7. After transferring to a cooling rack, cut into slices and serve.

Nutrition:

Calories: 144 Cal

Fat : 2 g

Carbohydrates: 27 g

Protein: 4 g

Fibre: 1 g

58. Saffron Tomato Bread

Preparation Time: 3 hours 30 minutes
Cooking Time: 15 minutes
Servings: 10
Ingredients:

- 1 teaspoon bread machine yeast
- 2½ cups wheat bread machine flour
- 1 Tablespoon paniharin
- 1½ teaspoon kosher salt
- 1½ Tablespoon white sugar
- Tablespoon extra-virgin olive oil
- Tablespoon tomatoes, dried and chopped
- 1 Tablespoon tomato paste
- ½ cup firm cheese (cubes)
- ½ cup feta cheese
- 1 pinch saffron
- 1½ cups serum

Directions:

1. Add 1 tablespoon of olive oil and the dried tomatoes five minutes before cooking. Mix in the tomato paste after adding it.
2. Fill the pan with all of the liquid and dry ingredients (except from the additives) and proceed with the bread machine's instructions.
3. Measure the ingredients carefully. To do this, use kitchen scales, a measuring cup, and a measuring spoon.

4. Choose MEDIUM for the crust type and BASIC for the baking programme.
5. Add the additives when the beep sounds or put them in the bread machine's dispenser.
6. Remove the bread from the pan by shaking it. Use a spatula if required.
7. After wrapping the bread in a kitchen towel, leave it alone for one hour. If not, a wire rack will work for cooling it.

Nutrition

Cholesterol: 20 g
Total Fat: 9.2g
Protein: 8.9 g
Sodium: 611 mg
Sugar: 5.2 g

59. Herb Bread

Preparation Time: 1 hour 20 minutes
Cooking Time: 50 minutes (20+30 minutes)
Servings: 1 loaf
Ingredients:

- 3/4 to 7/8 cup milk
- 1 tablespoon Sugar
- 1 teaspoon Salt
- tablespoon Butter or margarine
- 1/3 cup chopped onion
- cups bread flour
- 1/2 teaspoon Dried dill
- 1/2 teaspoon Dried basil
- 1/2 teaspoon Dried rosemary
- 11/2 teaspoon Active dry yeast

Directions:

1. Fill the bread pan with all the ingredients. Choose medium crust and proceed with the quick bake cycle. To begin, press Start.
2. See how the dough kneads after 5 to 10 minutes. If your machine makes straining noises or if the dough looks dry and hard, add one tablespoon of liquid at a time until the dough is smooth, pliable, soft, and a little tacky to the touch.
3. After baking, remove the bread from the pan. Before slicing, place on a rack and let cool for an hour.

Nutrition:
Calories: 65 Cal
Fat : 0 g
Carbohydrates: 13 g
Protein: 2 g

60. Original Italian Herb Bread

Preparation Time: 2 hours 40 minutes
Cooking Time: 50 minutes
Servings: 2 loaves
Ingredients:

- 1 cup water at 80 degrees F
- ½ cup olive brine
- 1½ tablespoons butter
- tablespoons sugar
- teaspoons salt
- 5 ⅓ cups flour
- teaspoons bread machine yeast
- 20 olives, black/green
- 1½ teaspoons Italian herbs

Directions:

1. Slice the olives.
2. Carefully follow the manufacturer's directions and add all the ingredients (except from the olives) to your bread machine.
3. Select French bread and Medium crust type in your bread maker's programme.
4. Press the Start button.
5. Add the olives when the maker beeps.
6. Wait until the entire cycle is finished.
7. After the loaf is done, remove the bucket and allow the loaf to cool for 5 minutes.
8. To take out the bread, gently shake the bucket.

9. After transferring to a cooling rack, cut into slices and serve.

Nutrition:

Calories: 386 Cal

Fat : 7 g

Carbohydrates: 71 g

Protein: 10 g

Fibre: 1 g

61. Cracked Black Pepper Bread

Preparation Time: 3 hours 30 minutes
Cooking Time: 15 minutes
Servings: 8
Ingredients:

- ¾ cup water, at 80°F to 90°F
- 1 tablespoon melted butter, cooled
- 1 tablespoon sugar
- ¾ teaspoon salt
- tablespoons skim milk powder
- 1 tablespoon minced chives
- ½ teaspoon garlic powder
- ½ teaspoon cracked black pepper
- cups white bread flour
- ¾ teaspoon bread machine or instant yeast

Directions:

1. Fill your bread maker with the ingredients according to the manufacturer's instructions.
2. Choose light or medium crust, programme the machine for Basic/White bread, and tap Start.
3. Take the bucket out of the machine after the bread is finished.
4. Give the bread five minutes to cool.
5. To remove the loaf, gently shake the bucket and place it onto a cooling rack.

Nutrition:
Calories: 141 calories;

Total Carbohydrate: 27 g
Total Fat: 2g
Protein: 4 g
Sodium: 215 mg
Fibre: 1 g

Cheese Bread

62. **Spinach and Feta Whole Wheat Bread**
Preparation Time: 10 Minutes
Cooking Time: 25 Minutes
Servings: 8
Ingredients:

- 2/3 cups whole wheat flour
- 1 1/2 tsp. instant yeast
- 1/4 cup unsalted butter, melted
- 1 cup lukewarm water
- tbsp. sugar
- 1/2 tsp. salt
- 3/4 cups blanched and chopped spinach, fresh
- 1/2 tsp. pepper
- 1/2 tsp. paprika
- 1/3 cup feta cheese, mashed

Directions:

1. 1 Preparing the Ingredients. Add all ingredients to the bread pan with the liquid-dry-yeast layering, excluding spinach, butter, and feta.
2. Place the pan inside the Zojirushi bread maker.
3. Choose the Bake cycle. Select Regular Whole Wheat. Hit the start button.

4. Gently fold in the feta and spinach when the dough has gathered.
5. Continue and wait for the loaf to finish cooking. After cooking, drizzle with butter.
6. After the bread is finished, the machine will enter the keep warm mode.
7. Allow it to remain in that state for 10 minutes or so before disconnecting it.
8. Take out the pan and let it cool for 10 minutes or more.

Nutrition:

Calories 174

Carbs 31.1g

Fat 3.1g

Protein 5.1g

63. **Cheese Loaf**
Preparation Time: 10 Minutes
Cooking Time: 25 Minutes
Servings: 8
Ingredients:

- ¼ cup flour
- tsp. instant yeast
- 1 3/4 cups water
- tbsp. sugar
- 1 1/2 cup shredded cheddar cheese
- tbsp. parmesan cheese
- 1 tsp. mustard
- 1 tsp. paprika
- tbsp. minced white onion
- 1/3 cup butter

Directions:

1. Start by adding all of the ingredients to the liquid-dry-yeast layer in the bread pan.
2. Position the pan inside the Zojirushi bread maker.
3. Choose the Bake cycle. To lighten the crust, use the Regular Basic Setting.
4. Select "Start" and watch the bread cook.
5. Upon completion of the bread, the machine will enter the keep warm mode.
6. After letting the bread sit in that state for roughly 10 minutes, disconnect it.

7. It might be a good idea to take the pan out at this point and give it 10 minutes to cool.

Nutrition:

Calories 174

Carbs 31.1g

Fat 3.1g

Protein 5.1g

64. Beer and Cheese Bread

Preparation Time: 10 Minutes

Cooking Time: 25 Minutes

Servings: 8

Ingredients:

- 3 cups bread or all-purpose flour
- 1 tbsp. instant yeast
- 1 tsp. salt
- 1 tbsp. sugar
- 1 1/2 cup beer at room temperature
- 1/2 cup shredded Monterey cheese
- 1/2 cup shredded Edam cheese

Directions:

1. Layer all the ingredients in the bread pan with liquid dry yeast, excluding the cheeses.
2. Put the pan into the Zojirushi bread maker.
3. Choose the Bake cycling. Select the Ordinary Basic Setting. Start by pressing Start.
4. Add the cheese just before the kneading is about to finish.
5. Wait until the bread is done.
6. After the bread is finished, the machine will enter the keep-warm mode.
7. Remember to disconnect it after allowing it to remain in that state for roughly 10 minutes.

8. Finally, take the pan out and give it 10 minutes or so to cool.

Nutrition:

Calories 174

Carbs 31.1g

Fat 3.1g

Protein 5.1g

65. Cheddar Cheese Basil Bread

Preparation Time: 10 Minutes
Cooking Time: 25 Minutes
Servings: 8
Ingredients:

- 1 cup milk
- One tablespoon melted butter cooled
- One tablespoon sugar
- One teaspoon dried basil
- ¾ cup (3 ounces) shredded sharp Cheddar cheese
- ¾ teaspoon salt
- cups white bread flour
- 1½ teaspoons active dry yeast

Directions:

1. Preparing the Ingredients. Put the ingredients into the bread maker from Zojirushi.
2. Choose the Bake cycle. Select light or medium crust, set the machine to Regular Basic, and press Start.
3. Take the bucket out of the machine if the loaf is finished.
4. Give the bread five minutes to cool.
5. To remove the loaf, gently shake the canister and place it onto a cooling rack.

Nutrition:
Calories 174|Carbs 31.1g|Fat 3.1g|Protein 5.1g

66. Double Cheese Bread

Preparation Time: 10 Minutes

Cooking Time: 25 Minutes

Servings: 8

Ingredients:

- 1¼ cups milk
- One tablespoon butter, melted and cooled
- Two tablespoons sugar
- One teaspoon salt
- ½ teaspoon freshly ground black pepper
- Pinch cayenne pepper
- 1½ cups (6 ounces) shredded aged sharp Cheddar cheese
- ½ cup (2 ounces) shredded or grated Parmesan cheese
- cups white bread flour
- 1¼ teaspoons bread machine or instant yeast

Directions:

1. Preparing the Ingredients. The ingredients should be added to your Zojirushi bread maker.
2. Press Start, choose light or medium crust, then program the machine to operate on a regular basis.
3. Now, take out the bucket from the machine if the bread is finished.
4. After 5 minutes, let the loaf cool.

5. To transfer the loaf, shake the bucket moderately.
6. It is placed onto a rack to cool as the final step.

Nutrition:

Calories 174

Carbs 31.1g

Fat 3.1g

Protein 5.1g

67. Herb and Parmesan Cheese Loaf

Preparation Time: 10 Minutes
Cooking Time: 25 Minutes
Servings: 8
Ingredients:

- cups + 2 tbsp. all-purpose flour
- 1 cup of water
- tbsp. oil
- tbsp. sugar
- tbsp. milk
- 1 tbsp. instant yeast
- 1 tsp. garlic powder
- tbsp. parmesan cheese
- 1 tbsp. fresh basil
- 1 tbsp. fresh oregano
- 1 tbsp. fresh chives or rosemary

Directions:

1. Layer the liquid cheese, dry yeast, and herb mixtures in the bread pan with all the ingredients.
2. Position the pan inside the Zojirushi bread maker.
3. Choose the Bake cycle. Opt for the Standard Basic Configuration.
4. Select "Start" and watch the bread cook.
5. Upon completion of the bread, the machine will enter the keep warm mode.

6. Just let it operate in that mode for 10 minutes or so before disconnecting.
7. Take out the pan and give it 10 minutes or so to cool.

Nutrition:

Calories 174

Carbs 31.1g

Fat 3.1g

Protein 5.1g

68. Garlic Parmesan Bread

Preparation Time: 5 Minutes
Cooking Time: 3 Hours and 45 Minutes
Servings: 10
Ingredients:

- Active dry yeast – ¼ oz.
- Sugar– 3 tbsp.
- Kosher salt – 2 tsp.
- Dried oregano – 1 tsp.
- Dried basil – 1 tsp.
- Garlic powder – ½ tsp.
- Parmesan cheese – ½ cup grated
- All-purpose flour   3 ½ cups
- Garlic – 1 tbsp., minced
- Butter – ¼ cup, melted
- Olive oil – 1/3 cup
- Water – 1 1/3 cups

Directions:

1. Put the garlic, butter, oil, and water in the bread pan.
2. Transfer the remaining ingredients to the bread pan, excluding the yeast.
3. Using your finger, make a small hole in the flour and add the yeast.
4. Ensure that there will be no liquids added to the yeast.
5. After choosing the basic setting, choose a light crust and get going.

6. After the loaf is finished, take the loaf pan out of the oven.
7. Let it cool down for 10 minutes.
8. 8 Cut into slices and serve.

Nutrition:

Calories 335

Carbs 37.7g

Fat 15.4g

Protein 9.7g

69. Cheese Buttermilk Bread
Preparation Time: 5 Minutes
Cooking Time: 2 Hours
Servings: 10

- Ingredients:
- Buttermilk – 1 1/8 cups
- Active dry yeast – 1 ½ tsp.
- Cheddar cheese – ¾ cup., shredded
- Sugar – 1 ½ tsp.
- Bread flour – 3 cups.
- Buttermilk – 1 1/8 cups.
- Salt – 1 1/2 tsp.

Directions.

1. According to the manufacturer's directions, add all ingredients to the bread machine pan.
2. Choose the basic bread setting, then press the light/medium crust button to get going.
3. Take out the loaf pan from the machine after the bread is finished.
4. Give it 10 minutes to cool.
5. Cut into slices and proceed to serve.

Nutrition:
Calories 182
Carbs 30g
Fat 3.4g
Protein 6.8g

70. **Gluten-Free Cheesy Bread**

Preparation Time: 5 Minutes
Cooking Time: 4 Hours
Servings: 10
Ingredients:

- Eggs – 3
- Olive oil – 2 tbsp.
- Water – 1 ½ cups.
- Active dry yeast – 2 ¼ tsp.
- White rice flour – 2 cups.
- Brown rice flour – 1 cup.
- Milk powder – ¼ cup.
- Sugar – 2 tbsp.
- Poppy seeds – 1 tbsp.
- Xanthan gum – 3 ½ tsp.
- Cheddar cheese – 1 ½ cups., shredded
- Salt – 1 tsp.

Directions:

1. Place the egg mixture, water, and oil in a bowl and transfer it to the bread machine pan.
2. Transfer the wet ingredient mixture into the bread pan and stir in the remaining ingredients in a large dish.
3. Choose the whole wheat option, then click "light/medium crust" to get started.
4. After the loaf is finished, take the loaf pan out of the oven.

5. Let it cool down for 10 minutes.
6. Slice into pieces and serve.

Nutrition:

Calories 317

Carbs 43.6g

Fat 11g

Protein 10.6g

71. Olive Cheese Bread

Preparation Time: 10 Minutes

Cooking Time: 25 Minutes

Servings: 8

Ingredients:

- 1 cup milk
- 1½ tablespoons melted butter, cooled
- One teaspoon of minced garlic
- 1½ tablespoons sugar
- One teaspoon salt
- cups white bread flour
- ¾ cup (3 ounces) shredded Swiss cheese
- One teaspoon bread machine or instant yeast
- 1/3 cup chopped black olives

Directions:

1. Getting the Ingredients Ready. Put the ingredients into your Zojirushi bread maker, making sure to mix the cheese and flour together first.
2. Select light or medium crust, program the machine for Regular Basic, and hit Start.
3. After the bread is finished, you can take the bucket out of the machine.
4. Give the bread 5 minutes to cool.
5. Shake the pot gently to remove the loaf, then remove it and place it on a rack to cool.

Nutrition:

Calories 174|Carbs 31.1g|Fat 3.1g|Protein 5.1g

72. Three Cheese Bread
Preparation Time: 10 Minutes
Cooking Time: 25 Minutes
Servings: 8
Ingredients:
- cups of bread or all-purpose flour
- 1 1/4 cup warm milk
- tbsp. oil
- tbsp. sugar
- 1 tsp. instant yeast or one packet
- 1 cup cheddar cheese
- 1/2 cup parmesan cheese
- 1/2 cup mozzarella cheese

Directions:
1. Getting the Ingredients Ready. Add all ingredients to the bread pan layered with liquid, and dry yeast.
2. Place the pan inside the Zojirushi bread maker.
3. Choose the Bake cycle. Select the Standard Basic Configuration.
4. Press the start button and watch the bread cook.
5. After the bread is finished, the machine will enter the keep warm mode.
6. Allow it to remain in that mode for 10 minutes or so before disconnecting.

7. After removing the pan, give it 10 minutes or so to cool.

Nutrition:

Calories 174

Carbs 31.1g

Fat 3.1g

Protein 5.1g

73. Chili Cheese Bacon Bread

Preparation Time: 10 Minutes
Cooking Time: 25 Minutes
Servings: 8
Ingredients:

- ½ cup milk
- 1½ teaspoons melted butter, cooled
- 1½ tablespoons honey
- 1½ teaspoons salt
- ½ cup chopped and drained green chiles
- ½ cup (2 ounces) grated Cheddar cheese
- ½ cup chopped cooked bacon
- cups white bread flour
- Two teaspoons bread machine or instant yeast

Directions:

1. Getting the Ingredients Ready. Fill your Zojirushi bread maker with the ingredients.
2. Choose the Bake cycle. Choose light or medium crust, set the machine to Regular Basic, and press Start.
3. From the machine, remove the bucket.
4. Let the loaf cool for half an hour.
5. To remove the loaf, gently swing the container and place it on a rack to cool.

Nutrition:
Calories 174|Carbs 31.1g|Fat 3.1g|Protein 5.1g

74. Cheese Pepperoni Bread

Preparation Time: 5 Minutes

Cooking Time: 2 Hours

Servings: 10

Ingredients:

- Pepperoni – 2/3 cup, diced
- Active dry yeast – 1 ½ tsp.
- Bread flour – 3 ¼ cups.
- Dried oregano – 1 ½ tsp.
- Garlic salt – 1 ½ tsp.
- Sugar – 2 tbsp.
- Mozzarella cheese – 1/3 cup., shredded
- Warm water – 1 cup+2 tbsp.

Directions:

1. Fill the bread machine pan with all the ingredients (except the pepperoni).
2. Choose the basic setting, then hit the start button after selecting medium crust.
3. Just before the last kneading cycle, add the pepperoni.
4. After the loaf is finished, take the loaf pan out of the oven.
5. Let it cool down for 10 minutes.
6. Slice and serve.

Nutrition:

Calories 176|Carbs 34.5g|Fat 1.5g|Protein 5.7g

75. Spinach and Feta Whole Wheat Bread
Preparation Time: 10 Minutes
Cooking Time: 25 Minutes
Servings: 8
Ingredients:
- 2/3 cups whole wheat flour
- 1 1/2 tsp. instant yeast
- 1/4 cup unsalted butter, melted
- 1 cup lukewarm water
- tbsp. sugar
- 1/2 tsp. salt
- 3/4 cups blanched and chopped spinach, fresh
- 1/2 tsp. pepper
- 1/2 tsp. paprika
- 1/3 cup feta cheese, mashed

Directions:
1. 1 Preparing the Ingredients. Add all ingredients to the bread pan with liquid-dry-yeast layering, excluding spinach, butter, and feta.
2. Second, place the pan inside the Zojirushi bread maker.
3. 3
4. Choose the Bake cycle. Select Regular Whole Wheat. Hit the start button.
5. Gently fold in the feta and spinach when the dough has gathered.

6. Continue and wait for the loaf to finish cooking. After cooking, drizzle with butter.
7. After the bread is finished, the machine will enter the keep warm mode.
8. Allow it to remain in that state for ten minutes or so before disconnecting it.
9. Take out the pan and let it cool for 10 minutes or more.

Nutrition:

Calories 174

Carbs 31.1g

Fat 3.1g

Protein 5.1g

76. Parmesan Tomato Basil Bread

Preparation Time: 5 Minutes
Cooking Time: 2 Hours
Servings: 10
Ingredients:

- Sun-dried tomatoes – ¼ cup, chopped
- Yeast – 2 tsp.
- Bread flour – 2 cups.
- Parmesan cheese – 1/3 cup, grated
- Dried basil – 2 tsp.
- Sugar – 1 tsp.
- Olive oil – 2 tbsp.
- Milk   ¼ cup.
- Water – ½ cup.
- Salt – 1 tsp.

Directions:

1. Fill the bread machine pan with all the ingredients (excluding the sun-dried tomatoes).
2. Choose the default setting, then press the start button after selecting medium crust.
3. Just before the last kneading cycle, add the sun-dried tomatoes.
4. Take out the loaf pan from the machine after the bread is finished.
5. Let cool for ten minutes.
6. Slice and serve.

Nutrition:
Calories 183
Carbs 20.3g
Fat 6.8g
Protein 7.9g

77. Moist Cheddar Cheese Bread

Preparation Time: 5 Minutes

Cooking Time: 3 Hours and 45 Minutes

Servings: 10

Ingredients:

- Milk – 1 cup
- Butter – ½ cup, melted
- All-purpose flour – 3 cups
- Cheddar cheese – 2 cups, shredded
- Garlic powder – ½ tsp.
- Kosher salt – 2 tsp.
- Sugar – 1 tbsp.
- Active dry yeast   1 ¼ oz.

Directions:

1. Fill the bread pan with milk and butter.
2. Transfer the remaining ingredients to the bread pan, excluding the yeast.
3. Punch a small hole in the flour with your finger, then add the yeast to the mixture.
4. Ensure that there will be no liquids added to the yeast.
5. Choose the basic setting, choose a light crust, and proceed.
6. After the loaf is finished, take the loaf pan out of the machine.
7. Give it 10 minutes to cool.
8. Slice and serve.

Nutrition:
Calories 337
Carbs 32.8g
Fat 17.7g
Protein 11.8g

Bread Machine Recipes

78. **Beet Bread**

Preparation Time: 1 hour and 10 minutes

Cooking Time: 35 minutes

Servings: 6

Ingredients:

- 1 cup warm water
- and ½ cup almond flour
- 1 and ½ cups beet puree
- tablespoons olive oil
- A pinch of salt
- 1 teaspoon stevia
- 1 teaspoon baking powder
- 1 teaspoon baking soda

Directions:

1. In a bowl, whisk together the flour, water, and pureed beets.
2. Add the remaining ingredients, thoroughly mix the dough, and transfer it into a loaf pan that has been lined.
3. After an hour of rising the mixture in a warm location, bake the bread for 35 minutes at 375 degrees F.
4. Slice, cool, and serve the bread.

Nutrition:

Calories 200|Fat 8|Fibre 3|Carbs 5|Protein 6

79. Artichoke Bread

Preparation Time: 10 minutes
Cooking Time: 30 minutes
Servings: 10
Ingredients:

- oz. canned artichoke hearts
- 1 garlic clove, minced
- 1 cup parmesan, grated
- 1 cup almond flour
- ½ teaspoon baking powder
- 1 and ½ cups warm water

Directions:

1. In a bowl, combine the flour, baking powder, and water; stir thoroughly.
2. Add the remaining ingredients, thoroughly mix the dough, and then pour it into a round pan that has been lined.
3. After baking the bread for 30 minutes at 360 degrees F, let it cool, cut it, and serve.

Nutrition:

Calories 211

Fat 12,

Fibre 3

Carbs 5

Protein 6

80. Vegetable Spoon Bread

Preparation Time: 10 Minutes

Cooking Time: 35 Minutes

Serving: 9

Ingredients:

- 1 (10-ounce) package of frozen chopped spinach, thawed
- and squeezed dry
- eggs, beaten
- 1 (8 ounces) can of cream-style corn
- 1 cup low-fat sour cream
- 1/4 cup margarine, melted
- 1 (8.50ounces) package of corn muffin mix

Directions:

1. Set the oven's temperature to 350 degrees F (175 degrees C).
   Grease a 9-inch square baking dish.
2. Blend the spinach, eggs, corn, sour cream, and margarine thoroughly in a large bowl. Add the dry cornbread mixture and stir. Spread evenly after dispensing into the pan that has been prepared.
3. Preheat the oven and bake for thirty-five minutes, or until the tops are firm and gently browned.

Nutrition:

Calories: 226

Total Fat: 12.2 g

Cholesterol: 53 mg
Sodium: 605 mg
Total Carbohydrate: 24.8 g
Protein: 5.9 g

81. Lime Bread

Preparation Time: 10 minutes
Cooking Time: 50 minutes
Servings: 8
Ingredients:

- 2/3 cup ghee, melted
- cups swerve
- eggs, whisked
- teaspoons baking powder
- 1 cup almond milk
- tablespoons lime zest, grated
- tablespoons lime juice
- cups coconut flour
- Cooking spray

Directions:

1. In a bowl, combine the flour, swerve, baking powder, and lime zest; stir.
2. Combine the lime juice with the remaining ingredients, excluding the cooking spray, in a different bowl and well toss.
3. Mix the two mixtures together, thoroughly whisk the batter, and transfer it into two loaf pans coated with cooking spray. Bake for fifty minutes at 350 degrees F.
4. Slice, let it cool, and serve the bread.

Nutrition:
Calories 203|Fat 7|Fibre 3|Carbs 4|Protein 6

82. Unleavened Cornbread

Preparation Time: 10 Minutes
Cooking Time: 25 Minutes
Serving: 12
Ingredients:

- 1 cup cornmeal
- 1 cup all-purpose flour
- 1/4 cup white sugar
- 1 teaspoon salt
- 1 egg
- 1/4 cup shortening, melted
- 1 cup milk

Directions:

1. Start by preheating the oven to 425 degrees F (220 degrees C).
   Muffin papers can be used or greased in a 12-cup muffin pan.
2. 2 Combine the flour, cornmeal, sugar, and salt in a sizable bowl.
   The egg, shortening, and milk should be added to the well that you have created. Mix until thoroughly combined. Fill muffin cups with batter by spooning it in.
3. Place the muffins in the oven and bake for 20 to 25 minutes, or until a toothpick inserted into the centre comes out clean.

Nutrition:

Calories: 150

Total Fat: 5.4 g
Cholesterol: 17 mg
Sodium: 209 mg
Total Carbohydrate: 22.2 g
Protein: 3.1 g

83. Cheesy Broccoli Bread

Preparation Time: 10 minutes
Cooking Time: 15 minutes
Servings: 2
Ingredients:

- Cooking spray
- 1 egg
- 1 tablespoon coconut flour
- 1 tablespoon almond flour
- 1 tablespoon almond milk
- 1 tablespoon butter, melted
- ¼ teaspoon baking powder
- A pinch of salt
- 1 tablespoon broccoli, chopped
- 1 tablespoon mozzarella, grated

Directions:

1. In a bowl, combine the almond flour, coconut flour, baking powder, salt, mozzarella, and broccoli, and stir.
2. Add the other ingredients (apart from the cooking spray) and thoroughly combine everything.
3. Spray cooking spray on a loaf pan, add the bread batter, bake for 15 minutes at 400 degrees F, let cool, and then serve.

Nutrition:

Calories 244|Fat 20|Fibre 4|Carbs 6|Protein 6

84. Cinnamon Asparagus Bread

Preparation Time: 10 minutes
Cooking Time: 45 minutes
Servings: 8
Ingredients:

- 1 cup stevia
- ¾ cup coconut oil, melted
- 1 and ½ cups almond flour
- eggs, whisked
- A pinch of salt
- 1 teaspoon baking soda
- 1 teaspoon cinnamon powder
- cups of asparagus, chopped
- Cooking spray

Directions:

1. 1 Combine all of the ingredients—aside from the cooking spray—in a bowl, and thoroughly whisk the mixture.
2. 2 Fill a loaf pan with this batter, spray it with cooking spray, bake it for 45 minutes at 350 degrees F, let it cool, cut it into slices, and serve it.

Nutrition:
Calories 165
Fat 6
Fibre 3
Carbs 5
Protein 6

85. Red Bell Pepper Bread

Preparation Time: 10 minutes
Cooking Time: 30 minutes
Servings: 12
Ingredients:

- 1 and ½ cups red bell peppers, chopped
- 1 teaspoon baking powder
- 1 teaspoon baking soda
- tablespoons warm water
- 1 and ¼ cups parmesan, grated
- A pinch of salt
- cups almond flour
- tablespoons ghee, melted
- 1/3 cup almond milk
- 1 egg

Directions:

1. In a bowl, combine the flour, baking soda, baking powder, parmesan, and bell peppers; whisk well.
2. Stir the bread batter thoroughly after adding the other ingredients.
3. Place it inside a loaf pan that has been lined, and bake it for thirty minutes at 350 degrees F.
4. Slice, serve, and let the bread cool.

Nutrition:
Calories 100|Fat 5|
Fibre 1|Carbs 4|Protein 4

86. Sauerkraut Rye Bread

Preparation Time: 5 minutes

Cooking Time: 3 hours

Servings: 1 loaf

Ingredients:

- 1 cup sauerkraut – rinsed and drained
- 3/4 cup warm water
- 1 ½ tablespoons molasses
- 1 ½ tablespoons butter
- 1 ½ tablespoons brown sugar
- 1 tsp caraway seed
- 1 ½ tsp salt
- 1 cup rye flour
- cups bread flour
- 1 ½ tsp active dry yeast

Directions:

1. Put all of the ingredients in the machine pan.
2. 2. Choose the basic bread setting.

Nutrition:

74 Calories

1.8 g total fat (0 g sat. fat)

4 mg Chol.

411 mg sodium

12 g carb

1 fibre

1.8 g protein

87. Great Plum Bread

Preparation Time: 10 minutes
Cooking Time: 50 minutes
Servings: 8
Ingredients:

- 1 cup plums, pitted and chopped
- 1 and ½ cups coconut flour
- ¼ teaspoon baking soda
- ½ cup ghee, melted
- A pinch of salt
- 1 and ¼ cups swerve
- ½ teaspoon vanilla extract
- 1/3 cup coconut cream
- eggs, whisked

Directions:

1. Combine the flour, baking soda, swerve, salt, and vanilla in a bowl and stir.
2. 2 Place the plums in another bowl and add the other ingredients, stirring to combine.
3. 3 Stir thoroughly to thoroughly blend the two ingredients.
4. 4 Fill two loaf pans with batter, then bake for fifty minutes at 350 degrees F.
5. 5 Let cool, then cut and serve the bread.

Nutrition:

Calories 199|Fat 8|Fibre 3|Carbs 6|Protein 4

88. Delicious Cantaloupe Bread

Preparation Time: 10 minutes
Cooking Time: 1 hour
Servings: 8
Ingredients:

- tablespoons stevia
- eggs
- 1 cup coconut oil, melted
- 1 tablespoon vanilla extract
- 1 teaspoon baking powder
- 1 teaspoon baking soda
- teaspoons cinnamon powder
- ½ teaspoon ginger, ground
- cups cantaloupe, peeled and pureed
- ½ cup ghee, melted
- cups almond flour

Directions:

1. In a bowl, combine the flour, stevia, baking powder, baking soda, ginger, and cinnamon.
2. Mix the batter thoroughly after adding the other ingredients.
3. Pour into two loaf pans that have been lined, and bake for one hour at 360 degrees F.
4. Slice, serve, and let the bread cool.

Nutrition:

Calories 211|Fat 8|Fibre 3|Carbs 6|Protein 6

89. **Vegan Cornbread**
Preparation Time: 10 Minutes
Cooking Time: 20 Minutes
Serving: 9
Ingredients:

- 1 cup all-purpose flour
- 1 cup cornmeal
- 1/4 cup turbinado sugar
- 1 tablespoon baking powder
- 1 teaspoon salt
- 1 cup sweetened, plain soy milk
- 1/3 cup vegetable oil
- 1/4 cup soft silken tofu

Directions:

1. 1. Set an oven thermometer to 400 degrees F, or 200 degrees Celsius.
   Grease a baking pan that is 7 inches square. In a mixing bowl, whisk together the flour, cornmeal, sugar, baking powder, and salt; set aside.
2. 2. Put the oil, tofu, and soy milk in a blender. After covering, purée until smooth. In the centre of the cornmeal mixture, create a well. Transfer the tofu that has been pureed into the well and mix in the cornmeal mixture until it becomes slightly moistened. Pour the mixture into the ready baking pan.

3. Bake for 20 to 25 minutes, or until a toothpick inserted into the centre comes out clean, in a preheated oven. Slice into 9 equal portions, and serve warm.

Nutrition:

Calories: 218

Total Fat: 9.1 g

Cholesterol: 0 mg

Sodium: 438 mg

90. Jalapeno Loaf

Preparation Time: 10 minutes
Cooking Time: 22 minutes
Servings: 6
Ingredients:

- 1 and ½ cups almond flour
- ½ cup flaxseed meal
- A pinch of salt
- teaspoons baking powder
- tablespoons butter, melted
- ½ cup sour cream
- eggs
- drops stevia
- jalapenos, chopped
- ½ cup cheddar, grated
- Cooking spray

Directions:

1. In a bowl, combine flour, cheese, stevia, jalapeños, baking powder, and flaxseed meal; whisk.
2. To make the dough, combine the remaining ingredients and stir.
3. Bake it for 22 minutes at 375 degrees F in a loaf pan that has been sprayed with cooking spray.
4. Slice, serve, and let the bread cool.

Nutrition:

Calories 300|Fat 20|Fibre 3|Carbs 4|Protein 12

91. **Dutch Oven Bread**

Preparation Time: 20 minutes

Cooking Time: 30 minutes

Servings: 6

Ingredients:

- 1 teaspoon baking powder
- 1 teaspoon baking soda
- cups almond flour
- 1 and ½ cups warm water
- A pinch of salt
- 1 teaspoon stevia

Directions:

1. In a bowl, thoroughly whisk the flour and water mixture.
2. Stir in the remaining ingredients until a dough forms, then set aside for 20 minutes.
3. Place the dough in a Dutch oven and bake for thirty minutes at 400 degrees Fahrenheit.
4. Slice, cool, and serve the bread.

Nutrition:

Calories 143

Fat 9

Fibre 3

Carbs 4

Protein 6

92. Keto Spinach Bread

Preparation Time: 10 minutes
Cooking Time: 30 minutes
Servings: 10
Ingredients:

- ½ cup spinach, chopped
- 1 tablespoon olive oil
- 1 cup water
- cups almond flour
- A pinch of salt and black pepper
- 1 tablespoon stevia
- 1 teaspoon baking powder
- 1 teaspoon baking soda
- ½ cup cheddar, shredded

Directions:

1. In a bowl, combine the flour, baking powder, baking soda, stevia, salt, and pepper; stir well.
2. Stir in the other ingredients thoroughly and transfer the mixture into a loaf pan that has been lined.
3. After 30 minutes of cooking at 350 degrees F, let the bread cool, then cut and serve.

Nutrition:

Calories 142|Fat 7|Fibre 3,|Carbs 5|Protein 6

93. Carrot Polenta Loaf

Preparation Time: 5 minutes
Cooking Time: 3 hours
Servings: 1 loaf
Ingredients:

- oz. lukewarm water
- tablespoons extra-virgin olive oil
- 1 tsp salt
- 1 ½ tablespoons sugar
- 1 ½ tablespoons dried thyme
- 1 ½ cups freshly grated carrots
- 1/2 cup yellow cornmeal
- 1 cup light rye flour
- ½ cup bread flour
- tsp instant active dry yeast

Directions:

1. Put all of the ingredients in the machine pan.
2. Select the dough setting.
3. Transfer dough onto a surface dusted with flour after the cycle is finished.
4. Knead dough until it forms an oval shape, then cover with plastic wrap and set aside to rest for ten to fifteen minutes.
5. Turn the bottom side up and flatten after resting.

6. Fold the upper third of the way to the lower third. The bottom should then be folded ⅓ of the way over the top.
7. Set the oven to 400 degrees.
8. Sprinkle cornmeal on a baking sheet, put the dough on it, and cover it to let it rise for 20 minutes in a warm location.
9. After the bread has risen, cut three large, diagonal cuts in its top and lightly mist it with cold water.
10. Bake for 20 to 25 minutes, or until beautifully browned.

Nutrition:

146 Calories

1 mg cholesterol

2 g total fat

186 mg sodium

27 g carb. 2 fibre

3.9 g protein

94. German Black Bread

Preparation Time: 3 hours 50 minutes

Cooking Time: 0

Servings: 10

Ingredients:

- 1 cup water plus 2 tablespoons water
- tablespoons apple cider vinegar
- tablespoons molasses
- 1 tablespoon sugar
- 1 teaspoon salt
- 1 teaspoon instant coffee
- ¼ teaspoon fennel seeds
- 1 tablespoon caraway seeds
- ½ ounce unsweetened chocolate
- ½ cup bran cereal flakes
- ½ cup bread flour
- ½ cup rye flour
- cups whole almond flour
- 1 package active dry yeast

Directions:

1. Start with the water and work your way through the list of ingredients for bread in your bread machine, ending with the yeast. Switch the bread maker to the whole wheat setting.

2. Make sure the dough is still a softball by checking on it after approximately 5 minutes. In case it's excessively dry, add 1 tablespoon of water at a time, and in case it's too wet, add flour 1 tablespoon at a time.
3. When the bread is cooked, let it cool on a cooling rack.

Nutrition:

Calories: 102

Carbs: 3.8 g

Fibre: 3.4 g

Fat: 1.4 g

Protein: 5.0 g.

95. Easy Cucumber Bread

Preparation Time: 10 minutes
Cooking Time: 50 minutes
Servings: 6
Ingredients:

- 1 cup erythritol
- 1 cup coconut oil, melted
- 1 cup almonds, chopped
- 1 teaspoon vanilla extract
- A pinch of salt
- A pinch of nutmeg, ground
- ½ teaspoon baking powder
- A pinch of cloves
- eggs
- 1 teaspoon baking soda
- 1 tablespoon cinnamon powder
- cups cucumber peeled, deseeded, and shredded
- cups coconut flour
- Cooking spray

Directions:

1. In a bowl, combine the flour, almonds, cucumber, salt, vanilla essence, cloves, cinnamon, baking soda, and baking powder. Stir well.

2. Add the remaining ingredients, excluding the coconut flour, combine thoroughly, and then pour the dough into a loaf pan that has been sprayed with cooking spray.
3. Bake for 50 minutes at 325 degrees F, then allow the bread to cool before slicing and serving.

Nutrition:

Calories 243

Fat 12

Fibre 3

Carbs 6

Protein 7

Vegetable Bread

96. **Spinach Bread**

Preparation Time: 2 hours 20 minutes

Cooking Time: 40 minutes

Servings: 1 loaf

Ingredients:

- 1 cup water
- 1 tablespoon vegetable oil
- 1/2 cup frozen chopped spinach, thawed and drained
- cups all-purpose flour
- 1/2 cup shredded Cheddar cheese
- 1 teaspoon salt
- 1 tablespoon white sugar
- 1/2 teaspoon ground black pepper
- ½ teaspoons active dry yeast

Directions:

1. Place all ingredients in the bread machine pan in the recommended manufacturing order. Activate the white bread cycle.

Nutrition:

Calories: 121 calories;

Total Carbohydrate: 20.5 g

Cholesterol: 4 mg

Total Fat: 2.5 g

Protein: 4 g

Sodium: 184 mg

97. Hawaiian Bread

Preparation Time: 10 minutes

Cooking Time: 3 hours

Serving Size: 1 ounce (56.7g)

Ingredients:

- 3 cups bread flour
- 2 ½ tablespoons brown sugar
- ¾ teaspoon salt
- Two teaspoons quick-rising yeast
- One egg
- ¾ cup pineapple juice
- Two tablespoons almond milk
- Two tablespoons of vegetable oil

Direction:

1. Fill the bread pan with all of the wet ingredients before adding the dry ingredients.
2. Select a light crust colour and put the bread maker in "Basic" or "Normal" settings.
3. Allow the mixer to complete the kneading, baking, and mixing cycles.
4. Remove the pan from the cooker.
5. Put the bread on a cooling rack.
6. Slice and serve the bread an hour later.

Nutrition:

Calories: 169 | Carbohydrates: 30g

Fat: 3g | Protein: 4g

98. Orange Date Bread

Preparation Time: 20 minutes

Cooking Time: 1.5 hours

Serving Size: 1 ounce (28.3g)

Ingredients:

- 2 cups all-purpose flour
- 1 cup dates, chopped
- ¾ cup of sugar
- ½ cup walnuts, chopped
- Two tablespoons orange rind, grated
- 1 ½ teaspoons baking powder
- One teaspoon of baking soda
- ½ cup of orange juice
- ½ cup of water
- One tablespoon of vegetable oil
- One teaspoon of vanilla extract

Direction:

1. Fill the bread pan with the wet ingredients first, followed by the dry ingredients.
2. Turn the bread maker on to the "Quick" or "Cake" setting.
3. Allow each cycle to come to an end.
4. After removing the pan from the machine, leave the bread in the pan for an additional 10 minutes.
5. Remove from the pan and allow the bread to cool fully before slicing.

Nutrition:
Calories: 80 | Carbohydrates: 14g
Fat: 2g | Protein: 1g

99. Beer Bread
Preparation Time: 10-15 minutes
Cooking Time: 2.5-3 hours
Serving Size: 2 ounces (56.7g)
Ingredients:

- 3 cups bread flour
- Two tablespoons sugar
- Two ¼ teaspoons of yeast
- 1 ½ teaspoons salt
- 2/3 cup beer
- 1/3 cup water
- Two tablespoons of vegetable oil

Direction:

1. Combine the water, beer, oil, salt, sugar, flour, and yeast in a pan.
2. Select the "Basic" or "Normal" setting and light to medium crust colour when turning on the breadmaker.
3. Allow the machine to finish all of its cycles.
4. Remove the pan from the oven.
5. Place the beer bread on a wire rack and let it cool for approximately one hour.
6. Slice into 12 pieces and proceed to serve.

Nutrition:
Calories: 130 | Carbohydrates: 25g
Fat: 1g | Protein: 4g

100. **Zero-Fat Carrot Pineapple Loaf**
Preparation Time: 20 minutes
Cooking Time: 1.5 hours
Serving Size: 1 ounce (28.3g)
Ingredients:

- 2 ½ cups all-purpose flour
- ¾ cup of sugar
- ½ cup pineapples, crushed
- ½ cup carrots, grated
- ½ cup raisins
- Two teaspoons of baking powder
- ½ teaspoon ground cinnamon
- ½ teaspoon salt
- ¼ teaspoon allspice
- ¼ teaspoon nutmeg
- ½ cup applesauce
- One tablespoon molasses

Direction:

1. The wet ingredients should be added to the bread pan before the dry ones.
2. Set your bread machine to the "Quick" or "Cake" option.
3. Let the machine finish all of its cycles.
4. Take the pan out of the machine, but before moving the bread onto a wire rack, give it another 10 minutes.
5. Before slicing, let the bread cool.

Nutrition:
Calories: 70 | Carbohydrates: 16g
Fat: 0g | Protein: 1g

101. Oatmeal Walnut Bread

Preparation Time: 15 minutes

Cooking Time: 1.5 hours

Serving Size: 1 ounce per serving

Ingredients:

- ¾ cup whole-wheat flour
- ¼ cup all-purpose flour
- ½ cup brown sugar
- 1/3 cup walnuts, chopped
- ¼ cup oatmeal
- ¼ teaspoon of baking soda
- Two tablespoons of baking powder
- One teaspoon salt
- 1 cup Vegan buttermilk
- ¼ cup of vegetable oil
- Three tablespoons aquafaba

Direction:

1. Add the wet ingredients to the bread pan first, then the dry ingredients.
2. Set your bread machine to the "Quick" or "Cake" mode.
3. Let the cycles finish.
4. Remove the pan from the oven.
5. After 10 minutes of waiting, take the bread out of the pan.
6. After the bread cools, cut it into slices and serve.

Nutrition:
Calories: 80 | Carbohydrates: 11g
Fat: 3g | Protein: 2g

102. Zero-Fat Carrot Pineapple Loaf

Preparation Time: 20 minutes
Cooking Time: 1.5 hours
Serving Size: 1 ounce (28.3g)
Ingredients:

- 2 ½ cups all-purpose flour
- ¾ cup of sugar
- ½ cup pineapples, crushed
- ½ cup carrots, grated
- ½ cup raisins
- Two teaspoons of baking powder
- ½ teaspoon ground cinnamon
- ½ teaspoon salt
- ¼ teaspoon allspice
- ¼ teaspoon nutmeg
- ½ cup applesauce
- One tablespoon molasses

Direction:

1. Place the liquid ingredients into the bread pan first, followed by the dry ingredients.
2. Select the "Cake" or "Quick" setting on your bread maker.
3. Allow the machine to finish all of its cycles.
4. Remove the pan from the oven, but before moving the bread onto a wire rack, let it sit for an additional 10 minutes.
5. Let the bread cool before slicing.

Nutrition:
Calories: 70 | Carbohydrates: 16g
Fat: 0g | Protein: 1g

103. Onion and Mushroom Bread

Preparation Time: 10 minutes

Cooking Time: 1 hour

Serving Size: 2 ounces (56.7g)

Ingredients:

- 4 ounces mushrooms, chopped
- 4 cups bread flour
- Three tablespoons sugar
- Four teaspoons fast-acting yeast
- Four teaspoons dried onions, minced
- 1 ½ teaspoons salt
- ½ teaspoon garlic powder
- ¾ cup of water

Direction:

1. Fill the bread pan with water, then top with all of the dry ingredients.
2. Select the bread machine's "Fast" cycle setting.
3. Wait till each cycle is finished.
4. Transfer the bread onto a wire rack after removing it from the pan.
5. Let the bread stand for an hour before slicing it into twelve pieces.
6. Each slice is served with two ounces of food.

Nutrition:

Calories: 120 | Carbohydrates: 25g

Fat: 0g | Protein: 5g

104. Sweet Potato Bread

Preparation Time: 10 minutes
Cooking Time: 3 hours
Serving Size: 2 ounces (56.7g)
Ingredients:

- 4 cups bread flour
- 1 cup sweet potatoes, mashed
- ½ cup brown sugar
- Two teaspoons yeast
- 1 ½ teaspoon salt
- ½ teaspoon cinnamon
- ½ cup of water
- Two tablespoons vegetable oil
- One teaspoon vanilla extract

Direction:

1. Place the wet ingredients into the bread pan first, and then the dry ingredients.
2. Use the bread machine in the "Normal" or "Basic" setting.
3. Choose the crust colour setting that is light or medium.
4. Remove the bread from the machine when the cycles are complete, and let it cool on a wire rack before slicing and serving.

Nutrition:
Calories: 111 | Carbohydrates: 21g
Fat: 2g | Protein: 3g

105. **Black Forest Loaf**

Preparation Time: 20 minutes
Cooking Time: 3 hours
Serving Size: 2 ounces (56.7g)
Ingredients:

- 1 ½ cups bread flour
- 1 cup whole wheat flour
- 1 cup rye flour
- Three tablespoons cocoa
- One tablespoon caraway seeds
- Two teaspoons yeast
- 1 ½ teaspoons salt
- One ¼ cups water
- 1/3 cup molasses
- 1 ½ tablespoon canola oil

Direction:

1. In the bread pan, combine the ingredients by adding the wet components first, then the dry ones.
2. Turn on the bread machine to the "Normal" or "Basic" option and adjust the crust colour.
3. Remove the bread from the machine when all of the cycles have finished.
4. Let the bread cool before slicing it.

Nutrition:

Calories: 136 | Carbohydrates: 27g
Fat: 2g | Protein: 3g

106. Mashed Potato Bread

Preparation Time: 40 minutes
Cooking Time: 2.5-3 hours
Serving Size: 2 ounces (56.7g) per slice
Ingredients:

- 2 1/3 cups bread flour
- ½ cup mashed potatoes
- One tablespoon sugar
- 1 ½ teaspoons yeast
- ¾ teaspoon salt
- ¼ cup potato water
- One tablespoon ground flax seeds
- Four teaspoons oil

Direction:

1. Add the potato water, oil, flax seeds, mashed potatoes, sugar, salt, flour, and yeast to the pan in that sequence.
2. Set the bread maker's settings to medium crust colour and press the "Basic" or "Normal" mode.
3. Allow the bread maker to complete each cycle.
4. Take the bread pan out of the machine.
5. Remove the bread from the pan with caution.
6. Place the bread on a wire rack and allow it to cool before slicing.

Nutrition:
Calories: 140
Carbohydrates: 26 g

107. Onion Potato Bread
Preparation Time: 1 hour 20 minutes
Cooking Time: 45 minutes
Servings: 2 loaves
Ingredients:
- tablespoon quick rise yeast
- cups bread flour
- 1 1/2 teaspoon seasoned salt
- tablespoon sugar
- 2/3 cup baked potatoes, mashed
- 1 1/2 cup onions, minced
- large eggs
- tablespoon oil
- 3/4 cup hot water, with the temperature of 115 to 125 degrees F
- (46 to 51 degrees C)

Directions:
1. Put the liquid ingredients in the pan. Add the dry ingredients, except the yeast. Form a shallow well in the middle using your hand and put the yeast.
2. Place the pan in the machine, close the lid and turn it on. Select the express bake 80 setting and start the machine.
3. Once the bread is cooked, leave on a wire rack for 20 minutes or until cooled.

Nutrition:
Calories: 160 calories;
Total Carbohydrate: 44 g
Total Fat: 2 g
Protein: 6 g

108. Beetroot Prune Bread

Preparation Time: 3 hours
Cooking Time: 30 minutes
Servings: 20
Ingredients:

- 1½ cups lukewarm beet broth
- 5¼ cups all-purpose flour
- 1 cup beet puree
- 1 cup prunes, chopped
- tablespoons extra virgin olive oil
- tablespoons dry cream
- 1 tablespoon brown sugar
- teaspoons active dry yeast
- 1 tablespoon whole milk
- teaspoons sea salt

Directions:

1. Gather all of your bread ingredients and your measurement tools (cup, spoon, and kitchen scales).
2. With the exception of the prunes, measure the ingredients into the pan carefully.
3. In accordance with your bread machine's instructions, add all of the ingredients to the bread bucket in the correct sequence.
4. Close the lid.
5. Choose MEDIUM for the crust colour and BASIC for your bread machine's programme.
6. Press the START button.

7. Add the prunes to the dough after the signal.
8. Wait till the program finishes.
9. After finishing, remove the bucket and allow it to cool for 5 to ten minutes.
10. Shake the loaf out of the pan and place it on a cooling rack to cool for half an hour.
11. Cut, present, and savour the aroma of aromatic freshly baked bread.

Nutrition:

Calories: 443 calories;

Total Carbohydrate: 81.1 g

Total Fat: 8.2 g

Protein: 9.9 g

Sodium: 604 mg

Fibre: 4.4 g

Sugar: 11.7 g

109. Curd Bread
Preparation Time: 4 hours
Cooking Time: 15 minutes
Servings: 12
Ingredients:
- ¾ cup lukewarm water
- 2/3 cups wheat bread machine flour
- ¾ cup cottage cheese
- Tablespoon softened butter
- Tablespoon white sugar
- 1½ teaspoon sea salt
- 1½ Tablespoon sesame seeds
- Tablespoon dried onions
- 1¼ teaspoon bread machine yeast

Directions:
1. Fill the pan with all of the dry and liquid ingredients, then proceed with your bread machine's directions.
2. Pay close attention to the ingredient measurements. To do this, use kitchen scales, a measuring spoon, and a measuring cup.
3. Select MEDIUM for the crust type and BASIC for the baking programme.
4. Adjust the recipe's flour and liquid measurements if the dough is too wet or too dense.

5. After the programme is finished, remove the pan from the bread maker and allow it to cool for five minutes.
6. Loaf out of the pan with a shake. When needed, use a spatula.
7. After wrapping the bread in a kitchen towel, leave it alone for sixty minutes.
   If not, a wire rack will work for cooling it down.

Nutrition:

Calories: 277 calories;

Total Carbohydrate: 48.4 g

Cholesterol: 9 g

Total Fat: 4.7g

Protein: 9.4 g

Sodium: 547 mg

Sugar: 3.3 g

110. Golden Potato Bread

Preparation Time: 2 hours 50 minutes
Cooking Time: 45 minutes
Servings: 2 loaves
Ingredients:

- teaspoon bread machine yeast
- cups bread flour
- 1 1/2 teaspoon salt
- tablespoon potato starch
- 1 tablespoon dried chives
- tablespoon dry skim milk powder
- 1 teaspoon sugar
- tablespoon unsalted butter, cubed
- 3/4 cup mashed potatoes
- 1 large egg, at room temperature
- 3/4 cup potato cooking water, with a temperature of 80 to 90
- degrees F (26 to 32 degrees C)

Directions:

1. Start by making the mashed potatoes. After peeling, place the potatoes in a saucepan. Add enough cold water to completely cover them. Bring the mixture to a boil by turning up the heat to high. After lowering the heat, cook the potatoes until they are soft. After cooking, transfer the potatoes to a basin and mash them. Till the potatoes are ready to be used, cover the bowl. Keep the cooking water

warm until it reaches the required temperature.

2. The following components should be added to the bread pan in that order: egg, mashed potatoes, butter, sugar, milk, chives, potato starch, salt, flour, and yeast.

3. After putting the pan inside, shut the lid. A switch for it. Select your chosen crust colour and the sweet setting. Turn on the heat source.

4. After the bread has baked, carefully remove the mould and allow it to cool on a wire rack.

5. Slice and serve.

Nutrition:

Calories: 90 calories;

Total Carbohydrate: 15 g

Total Fat: 2 g

Protein: 4 g

Protein: 4 g

111. Zucchini Herbed Bread

Preparation Time: 2 hours 20 minutes
Cooking Time: 50 minutes
Servings: 1 loaf
Ingredients:

- ½ cup water
- teaspoon honey
- 1 tablespoons oil
- ¾ cup zucchini, grated
- ¾ cup whole wheat flour
- cups bread flour
- 1 tablespoon fresh basil, chopped
- teaspoon sesame seeds
- 1 teaspoon salt
- 1½ teaspoon active dry yeast

Directions:

1. Carefully follow the manufacturer's directions and add all of the ingredients to your bread maker.
2. Select Basic/White Bread as the bread machine's programme, and Medium for the crust type.
3. Press the START button.
4. Wait until the cycle is finished.
5. After the loaf is done, remove the bucket and let it cool for 5 minutes.
6. To take out the bread, gently shake the bucket.

7. Place on a cooling rack, cut, and proceed to serve.
8. Enjoy!

Nutrition:

Calories: 153 Cal

Fat: 1 g

Carbohydrates: 28 g

Protein: 5 g

Fibre: 2 g

Fruit and Vegetable Bread

112. Strawberry Shortcake Bread
Preparation Time: 10 Minutes
Cooking Time: 25 Minutes
Servings: 8
Ingredients:

- 1/2 cups milk, at 80°F to 90°F
- Three tablespoons melted butter, cooled
- Three tablespoons sugar
- 1½ teaspoons salt
- ¾ cup sliced fresh strawberries
- 1 cup quick oats
- 2¼ cups white bread flour
- 1½ teaspoons bread machine or instant yeast

Directions:

1. Preparing the Ingredients. Fill your Hamilton Beach bread maker with the ingredients.
2. Select the Bake cycle. Select a light or medium crust setting, programme the machine for Whitbread, then tap Start.
3. Take the bucket out of the machine if the loaf is done.
4. Give the bread a five-minute cooling period. Shake the can slightly to extract the bread, then place it on a cooling rack.

Nutrition:
Calories 277
Cholesterol 9g
Carbohydrate 48.4g
Dietary Fibre 1.9g
Sugars 3.3g
Protein 9.4g

113. Sun Vegetable Bread

Preparation Time: 15 minutes
Cooking Time: 3 hours 45 minutes
Servings: 8 slices
Ingredients:

- 2 cups (250 g) wheat flour
- 2 cups (250 g) whole-wheat flour
- 2 teaspoons paniharin
- 2 teaspoons yeast
- 1½ teaspoons salt
- 1 tablespoon sugar
- 1 tablespoon paprika dried slices
- 2 tablespoons dried beets
- 1 tablespoon dried garlic
- 1½ cups water
- 1 TABLESPOON VEGETABLE OIL

Directions:

1. Select the 4- hour baking programme with a medium crust colour.
2. To achieve a soft and smooth bun, pay close attention to the dough's kneading stage.

Nutrition:

Calories 253;
Total Fat 2.6g;
Saturated Fat 0.5g;
Cholesterol 0g;
Sodium 444 mg;
Total Carbohydrate 49.6g;

Dietary Fibre 2.6g;
Total Sugars 0.6g;
Protein 7.2g

114. Curd Onion Bread with Sesame Seeds

Preparation Time: 10 minutes

Cooking Time: 3 hours 50 minutes

Servings: 8 slices

Ingredients:

- 3/4 cup water
- 3 2/3 cups wheat flour
- 3/4 cup cottage cheese
- 2 tablespoons softened butter
- 2 tablespoon sugar
- 1 ½ teaspoons salt
- 1 ½ tablespoon sesame seeds
- 2 tablespoons dried onions
- 1 ¼ teaspoons dry yeast

Directions:

1. 1. Fill the bread machine with the ingredients as directed by the manufacturer.

   I have this order, along with the ingredients.
2. Use the BASIC programme to bake.

Nutrition:

Calories 277;

Total Fat 4.7g;

Saturated Fat 2.3g;

Cholesterol 9g;

Sodium 547 mg;

Total Carbohydrate 48.4g;

Dietary Fibre 1.9g;

Total Sugars 3.3g; Protein: 9.4g

115. Blueberry Bread
Preparation Time: 3 hours 15 minutes
Cooking Time: 40- 45 minutes
Servings: 1 loaf
Ingredients:

- 1 1/8 to 1¼ cups Water
- 6 ounces Cream cheese, softened
- 2 tablespoons Butter or margarine
- ¼ cup Sugar
- 2 teaspoons Salt
- 4½ cups Bread flour
- 1½ teaspoons Grated lemon peel
- 2 teaspoons Cardamom
- 2 tablespoons Nonfat dry milk
- 2½ teaspoons Red star brand active dry yeast
- 2/3 cup dried blueberries

Directions:

1. Using the least amount of space in a bread pan, combine all ingredients except the dried blueberries. Initiate the process by pressing Start.
2. While you knead the dough, observe it. Add additional liquid, one tablespoon at a time, until the dough forms a ball that is soft, tender, and slightly sticky to the touch after 5

to 10 minutes if it is dry and hard or if the machine seems to be straining to knead it.

3. Add the dried cranberries as you feel inspired.
4. Take out the bread from the pan, put it on top of the cake, and let it cool when the bake cycle is over.

Nutrition:

Calories: 180 calories

Total Carbohydrate: 250 g

Fat: 3 g

Protein: 9 g

116. **Yeasted Carrot Bread**
Preparation Time: 10 Minutes
Cooking Time: 25 Minutes
Servings: 8
Ingredients:
- ¾ cup milk
- Three tablespoons melted butter, cooled
- One tablespoon honey
- 1½ cups shredded carrot
- ¾ teaspoon ground nutmeg
- ½ teaspoon salt
- 3 cups white bread flour
- 2¼ tcaspoons of dry yeast

Directions:
1. Get the ingredients ready. Put the ingredients into the bread maker made by Hamilton Beach.
2. Choose the Bake cycle. Press Start after setting the machine to make Rapid Bread.
3. Take the bucket out of the machine if the bread is finished.
4. Give the bread 5 minutes to cool.
5. To remove the loaf and try it out onto a rack to cool, gently shake the bucket.

Nutrition:
Calories 277
Cholesterol 9g
Carbohydrate 48.4g

Dietary Fibre 1.9g
Sugars 3.3g
Protein 9.4g

117. **Peaches and buttercream Bread**

Preparation Time: 10 Minutes
Cooking Time: 25 Minutes
Servings: 8
Ingredients:

- 3/4 cup canned peaches, drained and chopped
- 1/3 cup heavy whipping cream, at 80°F to 90°F
- One egg, at room temperature
- One tablespoon melted butter cooled
- Two 1/4 tablespoons sugar
- 1 1/8 tcaspoons salt
- 1/3 teaspoon ground cinnamon
- 1/8 teaspoon ground nutmeg
- 1/3 cup whole-wheat flour
- 2 2/3 cups white bread flour
- 1 1/6 teaspoons bread machine or instant yeast

Directions:

1. 1. Get the ingredients ready. Fill your Hamilton Beach bread maker with the ingredients.
2. Select the Bake cycle. Press Start after setting the crust type to light or medium and programming the machine for Whitbread.
3. Remove the bucket from the machine after the bread is finished.

4. Give the bread a five-minute cooling period.
5. Shake the bucket to get rid of the loaf, then turn it out onto a cooling rack.

Nutrition:

Calories 277
Cholesterol 9g
Carbohydrate 48.4g
Dietary Fibre 1.9g
Sugars 3.3g
Protein 9.4g

118. **Strawberry Shortcake Bread**
Preparation Time: 10 Minutes
Cooking Time: 25 Minutes
Servings: 8
Ingredients:
- 1/2 cups milk, at 80°F to 90°F
- Three tablespoons melted butter, cooled
- Three tablespoons sugar
- 1½ teaspoons salt
- ¾ cup sliced fresh strawberries
- 1 cup quick oats
- 2¼ cups white bread flour
- 1½ teaspoons bread machine or instant yeast

Directions:
1. Get the ingredients ready. Fill your Hamilton Beach bread maker with the ingredients.
2. Select the Bake cycle. Press Start after setting the crust type to light or medium and programming the machine for Whitbread.
3. Remove the bucket from the machine after the bread is finished.
4. Give the bread a five-minute cooling period.
5. Shake the bucket to get rid of the loaf, then turn it out onto a cooling rack.

Nutrition:
Calories 277
Cholesterol 9g

Carbohydrate 48.4g
Dietary Fibre 1.9g
Sugars 3.3g
Protein 9.4g

119. **Squash Carrot Bread**

Preparation Time: 15 minutes
Cooking Time: 3 hours 45 minutes
Servings: 8 slices
Ingredients:

- 1 small zucchini
- 1 baby carrot
- 1 cup whey
- 1 ½ cups (180 g) white wheat flour
- 3/4 cup (100 g) whole wheat flour
- 3/4 cup (100 g) rye flour
- 2 tablespoons vegetable oil
- 1 teaspoon yeast, fresh
- 1 teaspoon salt
- ½ teaspoon sugar

Directions:

1. Chop the zucchini and carrots into pieces that are about 8 to 10 mm (1/2 inch) in size.
2. Heat the vegetable oil in a frying pan and sauté the vegetables over medium heat until they are tender. Add salt and pepper to the vegetables if you'd like.
3. To help the veggies cool down more rapidly, transfer them to a flat platter. They cannot be added to the dough while still heated.
4. Now let the yeast dissolve in the serum.
5. Send all types of flour, yeast serum, sugar, and salt to the bakery.

6. In the Dough for the Rolls programme, knead the dough.
7. Mix the vegetables into the dough right before finishing the batch.
8. The dough will become more moist when the vegetables are added. Place the dough onto a heavily floured surface following the fermentation phase, which will take about an hour before the dough's bulk doubles.
9. Shape it into a loaf and place it in an oiled mould.
10. Use a food film to conceal the form, then leave it for one to eleven and a half hours.
11. Place the bread in the oven and preheat it to 450°F.
12. After the bread has baked for 15 minutes, carefully take it out of the mould. Place it on the grate and continue baking for an additional 15 to 20 minutes.

Nutrition:
Calories 220;
Total Fat 4.3g;
Saturated Fat 0.8g;
Cholesterol 0g;
Sodium 313 mg;
Total Carbohydrate 39.1g;
Dietary Fibre 4.1g;
Total Sugars 2.7g; |Protein 6.6g

120. Savory Onion Bread

Preparation Time: 10 Minutes
Cooking Time: 25 Minutes
Servings: 8
Ingredients:

- 1 cup water, at 80°F to 90°F
- Three tablespoons melted butter, cooled
- 1 1/2 tablespoons sugar
- 11/8 teaspoons salt
- Three tablespoons dried minced onion
- 1 1/2 tablespoons chopped fresh chives
- 3 cups white bread flour
- One teaspoon bread machine or instant yeast

Directions:

1. Get the ingredients ready. Fill your Hamilton Beach bread maker with the ingredients.
2. Select the Bake cycle. Press Start after setting the crust type to light or medium and programming the machine for Whitbread.
3. Remove the bucket from the machine after the bread is finished.
4. Give the bread a five-minute cooling period.
5. Shake the bucket to get rid of the loaf, then turn it out onto a cooling rack.

Nutrition:

Calories 277
Cholesterol 9g
Carbohydrate 48.4g

Dietary Fibre 1.9g
Sugars 3.3g
Protein 9.4g

121. Pineapple Coconut Bread
Preparation Time: 10 Minutes
Cooking Time: 25 Minutes
Servings: 8
Ingredients:

- Six tablespoons butter, at room temperature
- Two eggs, at room temperature
- ½ cup coconut milk, at room temperature
- ½ cup pineapple juice, at room temperature
- 1 cup of sugar
- 1½ teaspoons coconut extract
- 2 cups all-purpose flour
- ¾ cup shredded sweetened coconut
- One teaspoon of baking powder
- ½ teaspoon salt

Directions:

1. 1. Get the ingredients ready. Put the sugar, coconut extract, eggs, pineapple juice, coconut milk, and butter into your Hamilton Beach bread maker.
2. 2. Select the Bake cycle. Press START after programming the machine for Rapid Bread. Mix the flour, coconut, baking powder, and salt in a small bowl while the wet ingredients are combining. Add the dry ingredients once the initial mixing is complete and the machine has moved. Once the loaf has finished baking, remove the bucket from the

machine. Let the loaf cool for 5 minutes. To remove the loaf, give the pot a little shake, then place it on a rack to cool.

Nutrition:

Calories 277

Cholesterol 9g

Carbohydrate 48.4g

Dietary Fibre 1.9g

Sugars 3.3g

Protein 9.4g

122. **Tomato Onion Bread**

Preparation Time: 10 minutes

Cooking Time: 3 hours 50 minutes

Servings: 12 slices

Ingredients:

- 2 cups all-purpose flour
- 1 cup wholemeal flour
- ½ cup warm water
- 4 3/4 ounces (140 ml) milk
- 3 tablespoons olive oil
- 2 tablespoons sugar
- 1 teaspoon salt
- 2 teaspoons dry yeast
- ½ teaspoon baking powder
- 5 sun-dried tomatoes
- 1 onion
- ¼ teaspoon black pepper

Directions:

1. Get all required products ready. Cut the onion finely and cook it in a pan. Dice the ten sun-dried tomato halves.
2. Add all liquid ingredients to the bowl, dust with flour, and add the onions and tomatoes. Do not touch the liquid while you add the baking powder and yeast.
3. Choose the baking option and press the button. The bread machine will knead the

dough at low rates if you select the Bread with Additives programme.

Nutrition:

Calories 241;

Total Fat 6.4g;

Saturated Fat 1.1g;

Cholesterol 1g;

Sodium 305mg;

Total Carbohydrate 40g;

Dietary Fibre 3.5g;

Total Sugars 6.8g;

Protein 6.7g

123. **Peaches and buttercream Bread**

Preparation Time: 10 Minutes
Cooking Time: 25 Minutes
Servings: 8

Ingredients:

- 3/4 cup canned peaches, drained and chopped
- 1/3 cup heavy whipping cream, at 80°F to 90°F
- One egg, at room temperature
- One tablespoon melted butter cooled
- Two 1/4 tablespoons sugar
- 1 1/8 teaspoons salt
- 1/3 teaspoon ground cinnamon
- 1/8 teaspoon ground nutmeg
- 1/3 cup whole-wheat flour
- 2 2/3 cups white bread flour
- 1 1/6 teaspoons bread machine or instant yeast

Directions:

1. Get the ingredients ready. Fill your Hamilton Beach bread maker with the ingredients.
2. Select the Bake cycle. Press Start after setting the crust type to light or medium and programming the machine for Whitbread.
3. Remove the bucket from the machine after the bread is finished.
4. Give the bread a five-minute cooling period.

5. Shake the bucket to get rid of the loaf, then turn it out onto a cooling rack.

Nutrition:

Calories 277
Cholesterol 9g
Carbohydrate 48.4g
Dietary Fibre 1.9g
Sugars 3.3g
Protein 9.4g

124. Fragrant Orange Bread

Preparation Time: 5 Minutes
Cooking Time: 25 Minutes
Servings: 8
Ingredients:

- 1 cup milk,
- Three tablespoons of freshly clasped orange juice
- Three tablespoons sugar
- One tablespoon melted butter cooled
- One teaspoon salt
- 3 cups white bread flour
- Zest of 1 orange
- 1¼ teaspoons bread machine or instant yeast

Directions:

1. Get the ingredients ready. Fill the Hamilton Beach bread maker with the ingredients.
2. Select the Bake cycle. Press Start after setting the machine to bake Whitbread with a light or medium crust. When the loaf is finished, take the bucket out of the machine. Let the loaf cool for 5 minutes.
3. Shake the pan slightly to get the loaf out of it, then place it on a rack to cool.

Nutrition:

Calories 277
Cholesterol 9g

Carbohydrate 48.4g
Dietary Fibre 1.9g
Sugars 3.3g
Protein 9.4g

125. **Fruit Syrup Bread**

Preparation Time: 10 Minutes
Cooking Time: 25 Minutes
Servings: 8

Ingredients:

- 3 2/3 cups whole wheat flour
- 1 1/2 tsp. instant yeast
- 1/4 cup unsalted butter, melted
- 1 cup lukewarm water
- 2 tbsp. sugar
- 1/4 cup rolled oats
- 1/2 tsp. salt
- 1/2 cup of syrup from preserved fruit

Directions:

1. Get the ingredients ready. Mix the syrup with half a cup of water.
   Warm up till just warm. To make exactly one cup of water, add extra water.
2. Spread a layer of liquid-dry yeast over all the ingredients, excluding the butter and rolled oats.
3. Put the pan into the bread maker made by Hamilton Beach.
4. Fill the automatic dispenser with rolled oats.
5. Choose the Bake cycle. Opt for whole-wheat bread.
6. Select "Start" and watch the bread cook.
7. After cooking, brush the top with butter.

8. After the bread is finished, the machine will enter the keep warm mode.
9. Before unplugging, let it stay in that state for roughly ten minutes.
10. Take out the pan and give it 10 minutes or so to cool.

Nutrition:

Calories 277
Cholesterol 9g
Carbohydrate 48.4g
Dietary Fibre 1.9g
Sugars 3.3g
Protein 9.4g

126. Cranberry Yogurt Bread

Preparation Time: 10 Minutes
Cooking Time: 25 Minutes
Servings: 8
Ingredients:

- 3 cups + 2 tbsp. bread or all-purpose flour
- 1/2 cup lukewarm water
- 1 tbsp. olive or coconut oil
- 1 tbsp. orange or lemon essential oil
- 3 tbsp. sugar
- 3/4 cup yoghourt
- 2 tsp. instant yeast
- 1 cup dried dried cranberries
- 1/2 cup raisins

Directions:

1. Get the ingredients ready. Add all ingredients to the bread pan's liquid-dry yeast layer, excluding the raisins and cranberries.
2. Put the pan into the bread maker made by Hamilton Beach.
3. Fill the fruit dispenser with its contents.
4. 4. Choose the Bake cycle. Select white bread.
5. Press the start button and watch the bread cook.
6. After the bread is finished, the machine will enter the keep warm mode.

7. Before unplugging, let it remain in that mode for at least ten minutes.
8. Take out the pan and give it 10 minutes or so to cool.

Nutrition:

Calories 277
Cholesterol 9g
Carbohydrate 48.4g
Dietary Fibre 1.9g
Sugars 3.3g
Protein 9.4g

Dough Recipes

127. Sesame Almond Crackers
Preparation Time: 10 minutes
Cooking Time: 24 minutes
Servings: 8
Ingredients:
- Tbsp. unsalted butter, softened slightly
- egg whites
- ½ tsp. salt
- ¼ tsp. black pepper
- ¼ cups almond flour
- Tbsp. sesame seeds

Directions:
1. Preheat the oven to 350 F.
2. Beat the egg whites, butter, salt, and black pepper in a bowl.
3. Add the sesame seeds and almond flour and stir.
4. Form the dough into a rectangle by moving it between two pieces of parchment paper.
5. Transfer the dough to a sheet pan after removing the top parchment paper.
6. Use a pizza cutter to cut the dough into crackers.
7. Bake, rotating the tray halfway through, until brown, 18 to 24 minutes.
8. Serve.

Nutrition:
Calories: 299
Fat: 28g
Carb: 4g
Protein: 8g

128. Italian Pie Calzone

Preparation Time: 5 minutes
Cooking Time: 1 hour5 minutes
Servings: 12
Ingredients:

- 1 ¼ cups water
- 1 teaspoon salt
- 3 cups flour
- 1 teaspoon milk powder
- 1 ½ tablespoons sugar
- 2 teaspoons yeast
- ¾ cup tomato sauce for pizza
- 1 cup pepperoni sausage, finely chopped
- 1 ¼ cups grated mozzarella
- 2 tablespoons butter, melted

Directions:

1. Fill the bread maker's bucket with water, salt, sugar, soluble milk, bread baking flour, and yeast in the manufacturer's suggested order. Choose the Dough option.
2. After the cycle is finished, roll the dough out onto a surface that has been lightly floured to create a 45 by 25 cm rectangle. Move to a baking tray that has been gently greased.
3. Combine the mozzarella and diced pepperoni in a small bowl.
   Along the middle of the dough, spoon the pizza sauce in a strip.

Add the cheese and sausage stuffing.
4. Make diagonal incisions at the sides that are 1 ½ cm apart and retreat 1 ½ cm from the filling.
5. After moistening the filler with water, cross the strips over it.
   Spread some melted butter on it.
6. Bake at 360 degrees F for 35 to 45 minutes.

Nutrition:

Calories 247;

Total Fat 9.2g;

Saturated Fat 3.9g;

Cholesterol 22mg;

Sodium 590g;

Total Carbohydrate 32g;

Dietary Fibre 1.5g;

Total Sugars 2.8 g;

Protein 8.6g

129. No-Yeast Sourdough Starter

Preparation Time: 10 minutes
Cooking Time: 0 minutes
Servings: 64
Ingredients:

- cups all-purpose flour
- cups of chlorine-free bottled water, at room temperature

Directions:

1. In a large glass bowl, stir together the flour and water using a wooden spoon.
2. Cover the bowl with plastic wrap, set it in a warm spot, and stir it at least twice a day for three to four days, or until it becomes bubbly.
3. Before usage, mix the starting in a covered glass jar that you keep in the refrigerator.
4. Restock your starter by mixing equal parts flour and water, using the same amount as you withdrew.

Nutrition:

Calories: 14
Fat: 0g
Carbohydrates: 3g
Fibre: 0g
Protein: 0g

130. Chocolate Chip Scones

Preparation Time: 10 minutes
Cooking Time: 10 minutes
Servings: 8
Ingredients:

- cups almond flour
- 1 tsp. baking soda
- ¼ tsp. sea salt
- 1 egg
- Tbsp. low-carb sweetener
- Tbsp. milk, cream, or yoghourt
- ½ cup sugar-free chocolate chips

Directions:

1. Preheat the oven to 350 F.
2. Place the baking soda, salt, and almond flour in a bowl and stir.
3. Add the egg, milk, chocolate chips, and sweetener after that. Stir thoroughly.
4. Place the dough on parchment paper after balling it up with your fingers.
5. Create a big circle out of the dough with a rolling pin. Make eight triangles out of it.
6. Line a baking sheet with the scones and parchment paper, spacing them apart by about an inch.
7. Bake for 7 to 10 minutes, or until fragrant and gently browned.

8 Cool and serve.

Nutrition:
Calories: 213
Fat: 18g
Carb: 10g
Protein: 8g

131. **Pizza Basis**

Preparation Time: 10 minutes

Cooking Time: 1 hour 20 minutes

Servings: 2

Ingredients:

- 1 ¼ cups warm water
- 2 cups flour
- 1 cup Semolina flour
- ½ teaspoon sugar
- 1 teaspoon salt
- 1 teaspoon olive oil
- 2 teaspoons yeast

Directions:

1. Fill the bucket of the bread machine with all the ingredients in the manufacturer's suggested order. Choose the Dough program.
2. Use the dough as the pizza's base once it has risen.

Nutrition:

Calories 718;

Total Fat 4.4g;

Saturated Fat 0.6g;

Cholesterol 0mg;

Sodium 1173g;

Total Carbohydrate 145.6g;

Dietary Fibre 5.9g;

Total Sugars 1.5 g;

Protein 20.9g

132. Cheddar Crackers

Preparation Time: 10 minutes
Cooking Time: 55 minutes
Servings: 8
Ingredients:

- Tbsp. unsalted butter, softened slightly
- 1 egg white
- ¼ tsp. salt
- 1 cup plus 2 Tbsp. almond flour
- 1 tsp. minced fresh thyme
- 1 cup shredded sharp white cheddar cheese

Directions:

1. Preheat the oven to 300F.
2. Beat together the butter, egg white, and salt in a bowl.
3. Add the cheddar and stir until well combined, followed by the almond flour and thyme.
4. Using two pieces of parchment paper, spread the dough into a rectangular shape.
5. After removing the top parchment paper, put the dough on a sheet pan with the bottom parchment paper still attached.
6. Using a pizza cutter, slice the dough into crackers.
7. Bake, rotating the tray halfway through, until brown, 45 to 55 minutes.

8. Cool and serve.

Nutrition:

Calories: 200

Fat: 18g

Carb: 4g

Protein: 7g

133. **Iranian Flat Bread** (Sangak)
Preparation Time: 3 hours
Cooking Time: 15 minutes
Servings: 6
Ingredients:

- cups almond flour
- ½ cup warm water
- 1 Tbsp. instant yeast
- tsp. sesame seeds
- Salt to taste

Directions:

1. Using a bowl, mix 1 tablespoon of yeast with ½ cup warm water. Let it stand for five minutes.
2. Add one cup of water and salt. Wait an additional ten minutes.
3. Add the flour one cup at a time, followed by the rest of the water.
4. Work up the dough into a ball and cover it to rest for three hours.
5. Set the oven temperature to 480 degrees Fahrenheit.
6. Roll out the dough with a rolling pin and form it into six equal balls.
7. Each ball should be rolled into ½-inch thick circles.

8. Spread a piece of parchment paper onto the baking sheet and arrange the rolled circles over it.
9. Make two little holes in the centre with your finger, and then fill each one with two tsp of sesame seeds.
10. Cook for three to four minutes, then turn and continue baking for an additional two minutes.
11. Serve.

Nutrition:

Calories: 26

Fat: 1g

Carb: 3.5g

Protein: 0.7g

134. Savory Waffles

Preparation Time: 10 minutes

Cooking Time: 20 minutes

Servings: 4

Ingredients:

- eggs
- 1 tsp. olive oil
- ½ cup sliced scallions
- ¾ cup grated pepper Jack cheese
- ¼ tsp. baking soda
- Pinch salt
- Tbsp. coconut flour

Directions:

1. Preheat the waffle iron to medium heat.
2. Using a bowl, combine all the ingredients. Allow the batter to settle and stir again.
3. Depending on the size of the waffle iron, scoop ½ cup to 1 cup of batter and transfer it to the iron. Cook as directed by the maker.
4. Serve warm

Nutrition:

Calories: 183

Fat: 13g

Carb: 4g

Protein: 12g

135. Cauliflower Breadsticks

Preparation Time: 10 minutes
Cooking Time: 35 minutes
Servings: 8
Ingredients:

- cups riced cauliflower
- 1 cup mozzarella, shredded
- 1 tsp. Italian seasoning
- eggs
- ½ tsp. ground pepper
- 1 tsp. salt
- ½ tsp. granulated garlic
- ¼ cup Parmesan cheese as a topping

Directions:

1. Preheat the oven to 350 F. Grease a baking sheet.
2. 2 Beat eggs until well combined.
3. 3 In a food processor, combine riced cauliflower, mozzarella cheese, garlic, pepper, Italian seasoning, and salt; process on low speed to blend. Mix in the eggs.
4. After pouring the dough into the prepared cookie sheet, pat it down until it is ¼ thick all over the pan.
5. After baking for half an hour, sprinkle the breadsticks with the parmesan cheese.

6. For two to three minutes, place the breadsticks under the grill to allow the cheese to melt.
7. Slice and serve.

Nutrition:

Calories: 165

Fat: 10g

Carb: 5g

Protein: 13g .

137. **Pizza Dough**

Preparation Time: 10 minutes
Cooking Time: 1 hours 30 minutes
Servings: 2
Ingredients:

- 1 cup of warm water
- ¾ teaspoon salt
- 2 tablespoons olive oil
- 2 ½ cups flour
- 2 teaspoons sugar
- 2 teaspoons yeast

Directions:

1. 1. Load the bread maker with ingredients.
2. 2. Turn on the Dough programme and initiate the loop.
3. 3. Distribute the completed dough into a pan or form that has been oiled.
4. Stand for ten minutes.
5. 4. Set the oven's temperature to 400°F. Place the filling and the pizza sauce on top of the dough. Add some shredded cheese on top.
6. 5. Bake until the border is browned, 15 to 20 minutes.

Nutrition:
Calories 716;
Total Fat 15.7g;
Saturated Fat 2.3g;
Cholesterol 0mg;

Sodium 881g;
Total Carbohydrate 124.8g;
Dietary Fibre 5.1g;
Total Sugars 4.4 g;

Sourdough Bread

138. Pumpernickel Bread

Preparation Time: 2 hours 10 minutes

Cooking Time: 50 minutes

Servings: 1 loaf

Ingredients:

- 1 1/8 cups warm water
- 1 ½ tablespoons vegetable oil
- 1/3 cup molasses
- tablespoons cocoa
- 1 tablespoon caraway seed (optional)
- 1 ½ teaspoon salt
- 1 ½ cups of bread flour
- 1 cup of rye flour
- 1 cup whole wheat flour
- 1 ½ tablespoons of vital wheat gluten (optional)
- 2 ½ teaspoon of bread machine yeast

Directions:

1. Fill the bread machine pan with all the ingredients.
2. Select the basic bread cycle.
3. Remove the bread to cool and enjoy!

Nutrition:

Calories: 97 Cal

Fat: 1 g

Carbohydrates: 19 g |Protein: 3 g

139. Honey Sourdough Bread

Preparation Time: 15 minutes; 1 week (Starter)
Cooking Time: 3 hours
Servings: 1 loaf
Ingredients:

- 2/3 cup sourdough starter
- 1/2 cup water
- 1 tablespoon vegetable oil
- tablespoons honey
- 1/2 teaspoon salt
- 1/2 cup high protein wheat flour
- cups bread flour
- 1 teaspoon active dry yeast

Directions:

1. Measure 1 cup of starter and remaining bread ingredients, add to bread machine pan.
2. For the basic/white bread cycle, select a medium or light crust colour.

Nutrition:

Calories: 175 calories;
Total Carbohydrate: 33 g
Total Fat: 0.3 g
Protein: 5.6 g
Sodium: 121 mg
Fibre: 1.9 g

140. **Sourdough Boule**

Preparation Time: 4 hours

Cooking Time: 25-35 minutes

Servings: 12

Ingredients:

- 275g Warm Water
- 500g sourdough starter
- 550g all-purpose flour
- 20g Salt

Directions:

1. Mix the flour, warm water, and starter together, then cover and leave to rest for at least half an hour.
2. After allowing it to sit, remove the dough onto a floured surface and whisk in the salt. It's going to be very sticky, but not too bad. The best way to flatten the dough is to "slap" it onto the counter, and then fold it in half several times.
3. After covering, let the dough rise. A few more times, do the slap and fold technique. After covering the dough, give it two to four hours to rise.
4. Gently pull the dough until the top is taught, or at least doubled in size. Repeat many times. Again, let it rise for two to four hours.
5. Set the oven's temperature to 475 F and preheat it using a baking stone or a cast-iron

pan. After the dough has risen, place it on the pot or stone and score the top many times. Bake for another 25 to 35 minutes after reducing the heat to 425 F after 20 minutes. It will be golden brown for the boule.

Nutrition:

Calories: 243 Cal

Fat: 0.7 g

Protein: 6.9 g

141. Garlic and Herb Flatbread Sourdough

Preparation Time: 1 hour

Cooking Time: 25- 30 minutes

Servings: 12

Ingredients:

- Dough
- 1 cup sourdough starter, fed or unfed
- 3/4 cup warm water
- teaspoons instant yeast
- cups all-purpose flour
- 1 1/2 teaspoons salt
- tablespoons olive oil
- Topping
- 1/2 teaspoon dried thyme
- 1/2 teaspoon dried oregano
- 1/2 teaspoon dried marjoram
- 1 teaspoon garlic powder
- 1/4 teaspoon onion powder
- 1/4 teaspoon salt
- 1/4 teaspoon pepper
- 3 tablespoons olive oil

Directions:

1. In the bowl of a stand mixer, combine all the dough ingredients and knead until smooth. Transfer to a bowl that has been lightly oiled, and allow it to rise for at least one hour. Punch down, then allow to rise again for a minimum of sixty minutes.

2. In a small dish, combine all topping ingredients except olive oil.
3. Gently grease a normal baking sheet or 9x13 baking pan, then pat and roll the dough into a long rectangle to fit within. Drizzle the dough with olive oil, then top with the herb and spice blend. For fifteen to twenty minutes, cover and allow to rise.
4. Bake for 25 to 30 minutes after preheating the oven to 425 degrees.

Nutrition:

Calories: 89 Cal

Fat: 3.7 g

Protein: 1.8 g

142. Herbed Baguette

Preparation Time: 45 minutes
Cooking Time: 20-25 minutes
Servings: 12
Ingredients:

- 1 1/4 cups warm water
- cups sourdough starter, either fed or unfed
- to 5 cups all-purpose flour
- 2 1/2 teaspoons salt
- 2 teaspoons sugar
- 1 tablespoon instant yeast
- 1 tablespoon fresh oregano, chopped
- 1 teaspoon fresh rosemary, chopped
- 1 tablespoon fresh basil, chopped
- Any other desired herbs

Directions:

1. Combine all ingredients in the bowl of a stand mixer; knead with a dough hook (or your hands) for 7 to 10 minutes, or until a smooth dough forms. Add extra flour if necessary.
2. Put the dough in a bowl that has been oiled, cover it, and let it rise for about two hours.
3. Pinch the dough and separate it into three equal portions. Each dough piece should be shaped into a baguette that is roughly 16 inches long. One way to accomplish this is to

roll the dough into a log, fold it, roll it again, and fold it again.

4. Roll out the baguette dough and place it on baking sheets with liners. Allow to rise for one hour.

5. Bake for 20 to 25 minutes after preheating the oven to 425°F.

Nutrition:

Calories: 197 Cal

Fat: 0.6 g

Protein: 5.8 g

143. Olive and Garlic Sourdough Bread
Preparation Time: 15 minutes; 1 week (Starter)
Cooking Time: 3 hours
Servings: 1 loaf
Ingredients:
- cups sourdough starter
- cups flour
- tablespoons olive oil
- tablespoons sugar
- 2 teaspoon salt
- 1/2 cup chopped black olives
- cloves chopped garlic

Directions.
1. Fill the bread machine pan with the starter and bread ingredients.
2. Select the dough cycle.
3. Conventional Oven:
4. Set the oven's temperature to 350.
5. Add more flour if the dough is sticky after the cycle is finished.
6. Form dough into a loaf pan or place onto a baking sheet.
7. Bake until golden, 35 to 45 minutes.
8. Let it cool before cutting.

Nutrition:
Calories: 150 calories;
Total Carbohydrate: 26.5 g
Total Fat: 0.5 g

Protein: 3.4 g
Sodium: 267 mg
Fibre: 1.1 g

144. Crusty Sourdough Bread
Preparation Time: 15 minutes
Cooking Time: 3 hours
Servings: 1 loaf
Ingredients:
- 1/2 cup water
- cups bread flour
- tablespoons sugar
- 1 ½ teaspoon salt
- 1 teaspoon bread machine or quick active dry yeast

Directions:
1. Measure 1 cup of starter and remaining bread ingredients, add to bread machine pan.
2. Choose a basic/white bread cycle with medium or light crust colour.

Nutrition:
Calories: 165 calories;
Total Carbohydrate: 37 g
Total Fat: 0 g
Protein: 5 g
Sodium: 300 mg
Fibre: 1 g

145. **Dinner Rolls**

Preparation Time: 3 hours
Cooking Time: 5-10 minutes
Servings: 24 rolls
Ingredients:

- 1 cup sourdough starter
- 1 1/2 cups warm water
- 1 tablespoon yeast
- 1 tablespoon salt
- tablespoons sugar
- 2 tablespoons olive oil
- cups all-purpose flour
- 2 tablespoons butter, melted

Directions:

- Combine the water, yeast, salt, sugar, oil, and sourdough starter in a big bowl. Whisk in the flour and continue to whisk until a dough forms. Increase the flour if necessary. After placing the dough in a bowl that has been buttered, give it 2 hours to double in size.
- After removing the dough from the bowl, cut it into pieces that are 2-3 inches in size. The buns should rise for about an hour while covered in a 9x13 pan that has been oiled.
- Bake the rolls for 15 minutes after preheating the oven to 350 F. After taking out of the oven, bake for a further five to ten minutes while brushing with melted butter.

Nutrition:
Calories: 128 Cal
Fat: 2.4 g
Protein: 3.2 g
Sugar: 1.1 g

Buns and Bread

146. Keto Monterey Jack Jalapeno Bread
Preparation Time: 15 minutes
Cooking Time: 0
Servings: 12
Ingredients:
- 1 cup water
- tbsps. non-fat milk
- 1 ½ tbsps. sugar
- 1 ½ tsp. salt
- 1 ½ tbsps. butter, cubed
- ¼ cup Monterey Jack cheese, shredded
- 1 small jalapeno pepper
- cups almond flour
- tsp. active dry yeast

Directions:
1. Remove the jalapeño's seeds and stem, then chop it finely.
2. Add the ingredients mentioned above to the bread machine pan.
3. Close the lid, choose the light or medium CRUST COLOUR and the BASIC cycle, then press START.
4. Before slicing, place the loaf on a cooling rack when the cycle is finished.
5. Serve as an accompaniment to your preferred main meal or salad.

Nutrition:
Calories: 47
Calories from fat: 27
Total Fat: 3 g
Total Carbohydrates: 3 g
Net Carbohydrates: 2 g
Protein: 2 g

147. Mustard Beer Bread

Preparation Time: 3 hours

Cooking Time: 0

Servings: 8

Ingredients:

- 1 ¼ cups dark beer
- 1/3 cups flour
- ¾ cup wholemeal flour
- 1 tablespoon olive oil
- teaspoons mustard seeds
- 1 ½ teaspoons dry yeast
- 1 teaspoon salt
- teaspoons brown sugar

Directions:

1. To release the gas from a beer bottle, open it and leave it for half an hour.
2. Combine the beer, butter, mustard seeds, sifted flour, and wholemeal flour in the bucket of a bread machine.
3. Add sugar and salt to the bucket at various angles. Toss the mustard seeds into the groove you made in the middle of the flour.
4. Start the baking program.

Nutrition:

Carbohydrates 4.2 g

Fats 1 g

Protein 4.1 g

Calories 118

148. Gluten-Free Chocolate Zucchini Bread
Preparation Time: 5 minutes
Cooking Time: 0
Servings: 12
Ingredients:

- 1 ½ cups coconut flour
- ¼ cup unsweetened cocoa powder
- ½ cup erythritol
- ½ tsp cinnamon
- 1 tsp baking soda
- 1 tsp baking powder
- ¼ tsp salt
- ¼ cup coconut oil, melted
- eggs
- 1 tsp vanilla
- cups zucchini, shredded

Directions:

1. After stripping the zucchini, pat dry with paper towels and lay aside.
2. Add lightly beaten eggs and coconut oil to the pan of the bread machine.
3. Pour the remaining mixture into the pan.
4. Adjust the bread maker to be gluten-free.
5. After the bread is finished, take the pan out of the bread maker.

6. Let cool somewhat before moving to a cooling rack.
7. Your bread will be kept for up to five days in storage.

Nutrition:

Calories 185
Carbohydrates 6 g
Fats 17 g
Protein 5 g

149. **Keto Rye Sandwich Bread**
Preparation Time: 10 minutes
Cooking Time: 3 hours
Servings: 12
Ingredients:

- ¼ cups warm water
- 2 tbsps. melted butter, unsalted
- 2 tsp. white sugar
- 1 ½ tsp. salt
- 1 tbsp. baking powder
- ¼ tsp. ground ginger
- ¼ cup granulated swerve
- cups of vital wheat gluten
- cups of super fine almond flour
- ¼ cup dark rye flour
- 1 tsp. Active dry yeast
- 1 tbsp. caraway seeds

Directions:

1. Fill the bread machine bucket with all of the ingredients, then cover it.
2. On your bread machine, select the WHOLE WHEAT cycle and pick a light colour for CRUST COLOUR. Click the START button.
3. After the cycle has finished, take the pan out of the bread maker and place the loaf on a cooling rack.
4. To serve, slice and assemble a pastrami or Rueben sandwich.

Nutrition:
Calories: 275
Calories from fat: 144
Total Fat: 16 g
Total Carbohydrates: 12
Net Carbohydrates: 8 g
Protein: 22 g

150. Swiss Wholemeal Cheese Bread

Preparation Time: 3 hours

Cooking Time: 0

Servings: 8

Ingredients:

- ¾ cup warm water
- 1 tablespoon sugar
- 1 teaspoon salt
- tablespoons green cheese
- 1 cup flour
- 9/10 cup flour whole-grain, finely ground
- 1 teaspoon yeast
- 1 teaspoon paprika

Directions:

1. The ingredients are given in the bread machine's order of placement.
2. At the signal, add the paprika.
3. The grey bread has a pulp that is porous. Additionally, it doesn't go bad quickly. It tastes distinct and has intriguing cheese notes.

Nutrition:

Carbohydrates 5 g

Fats 1 g

Protein 4.1 g

Calories 118

151. Keto Flaxseed Honey Bread

Preparation Time: 10 minutes
Cooking Time: 20 minutes
Servings: 18 slices
Ingredients:

- 1 cup warm water
- small eggs, lightly beaten
- ½ cup oat fibre
- 2/3 cup flaxseed meal
- 1.25 cup vital wheat gluten
- 1 tsp. salt
- tbsp. swerve powdered sweetener
- 1 tsp. honey
- ½ tsp. xanthan gum
- tbsps. Butter, unsalted
- 1 tbsp. dry active yeast

Directions:

1. Fill the bread bucket with water.
2. In that order, add the eggs, honey, erythritol, salt, xanthan, flaxseed meal, oat fibre, and wheat gluten. Add the yeast and the softened butter.
3. Place the bread bucket in your bread maker and close the cover.
   After choosing BASIC, choose CRUST COLOUR > Medium Darkness.
   Once the bread starts to cook, press the START button.

4. Before slicing, let the bread cool on a cooling rack.
5. Serve with your preferred grilled meat or chicken. Keep in mind that the nutrition information only applies to the bread.

Nutrition:

Calories: 96
Calories from fat: 36
Total Fat: 4 g
Total Carbohydrates: 5 g
Net Carbohydrates: 3 g
Protein: 8 g

152. Basic Sweet Yeast Bread

Preparation Time: 3 hours
Cooking Time: 0
Servings: 8
Ingredients:

- 1 egg
- ¼ cup butter
- 1/3 cup sugar
- 1 cup milk
- ½ teaspoon salt
- cups almond flour
- 1 tablespoon active dry yeast
- After beeping:
- fruits/ground nuts

Directions:

1. Carefully follow the manufacturer's directions and add all ingredients (except fruits and ground nuts) to your bread machine.
2. Select LIGHT or MEDIUM for the crust type and set your bread machine's program to BASIC/SWEET.
3. Press the START button.
4. Add fruits or ground nuts after the machine sounds.
5. Wait until the entire cycle is finished.
6. After the loaf is done, remove the bucket and allow the bread to cool for five minutes.

7. To get the bread out of the bucket, gently shake it.
8. Transfer it to a cooling rack, cut it into slices, and serve.
9. Enjoy!

Nutrition:

Carbohydrates 2.7 g

Fats 7.6 g

Protein 8.8 g

Calories 338

153. Buns with Cottage Cheese
Preparation Time: 10 minutes
Cooking Time: 15 minutes
Servings: 8
Ingredients:
- eggs
- oz. Almond flour
- 1 oz. Erythritol
- 1/8 tsp. Stevia
- cinnamon and vanilla extract to taste

Filling:
- ½ oz. Cottage cheese
- 1 egg
- cinnamon and vanilla extract to taste

Directions:
1. Mix the ingredients for the filling in a bowl to prepare it..
2. Blend almond flour and eggs together until smooth. Taste and add erythritol, stevia, and flavours.
3. Spoon 1 tablespoon. Press dough into silicone moulds. Use roughly 1 tsp of spooning. Cover with filling and bake for 15 minutes at 365°F.

Nutrition:
Calories: 77
Fat: 5.2g
Carb: 6.7g |Protein: 5.8g

154. Keto Orange Cranberry Bread
Preparation Time: 10 minutes
Cooking Time: 0
Servings: 10
Ingredients:

- ¼ cup almond flour
- 1 tbsp. baking powder
- ¼ tsp. kosher salt
- large eggs
- 1 ½ cup buttermilk
- tbsp. canola oil
- 1 ½ cup brown sugar
- ½ tbsp. vanilla
- ½ tsp. nutmeg
- ¾ tsp. orange zest
- tbsp. orange juice, fresh
- 1 cup fresh cranberries, chopped

Directions:

1. Fill your bread machine bucket with all of the ingredients, excluding the cranberries.
2. Turn off the bread maker and close it before choosing the QUICK BREAD option and pressing START.
3. Add the chopped cranberries and open the lid after you hear the ping or the fruit and nut indication. To proceed, replace the cover and press START.

4. Move the loaf to a wire rack and allow it to cool after the cycle is complete.
5. Slice, then present with your preferred salad.

Nutrition:

Calories: 141

Calories from fat: 110

Total Fat: 12 g

Total Carbohydrates: 5 g

Net Carbohydrates: 4 g

Protein: 4 g

Dear Valued customer,

I hope you're enjoying the book you just bought! I appreciate your support and am happy that you chose to purchase my product.

I am aware of how valuable your time is, and I would appreciate any additional time you could spare to give a frank assessment. I think consumer input is priceless, and I can make future products even better with your aid.

If you could take a few minutes to provide an unbiased review of this book, I would be eternally grateful. Your opinions and input are appreciated, and I would be grateful to hear your suggestions on how I might be able to do better.
I value your dedication to my product and am grateful you took the time to write a frank review.

Best Regards

Conclusion

Some of the simplest and tastiest bread recipes you'll find are in this book.

There's no need to order any ingredients or visit any specialty stores because these loaves of bread are produced with common components that you can obtain locally. You can have the same meals you used to like and follow your diet as closely as you like with these bread pieces.

In addition, we now know how important it is to have a bread maker in our kitchen. Using it is relatively easy. All you have to know is how it works and its features. To become familiar with the machine's dos and don'ts, you should also utilise it more frequently.

To use the bread maker correctly, you must follow the instructions found in the manual. The directions differ according to the brand and model, and there is a certain method for loading the ingredients that needs to be followed. Upon receiving a machine, it is recommended that you take the time to thoroughly read the instructions so that you can maximise its functionality and achieve superior outcomes. The recipe book will specify exactly what to put in it and the settings to use based on the various components and bread kind you choose to make.

A bread maker in your home simplifies things. Whether you are a home cook or a professional baker, this tool will help you get the best bread flavours and textures with the least amount of work. Making bread is an art, and even if you're not an expert, you can still create beautiful bread by using a bread machine that allows you to work with a certain sort of flour with extra care and special technique. We have covered every type of bread maker in this book, along with practical uses for them. To help all the novices understand how to deal with the main ingredients of bread and what variety to use to obtain a specific type of bread, basic knowledge about flour and yeast is also covered. Lastly, some delectable bread recipes were provided for you to try at home.

Printed by Amazon Italia Logistica S.r.l.
Torrazza Piemonte (TO), Italy

56980943R00167